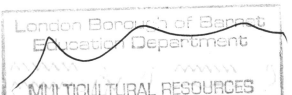
Fax 020 8201 3018
slrs@barnet.gov.uk

D1626654

BLACK HISTORY RESOURCE WORKING GROUP MEMBERS

Lenford White (Editor)
*Assistant Education Officer in Liverpool Education Directorate's
Race Equality Management Team - Liverpool City Council.*

Paulette Clunie
*African/Caribbean Librarian, Multi-Racial Library Promotion Unit,
Leisure Services Directorate Liverpool City Council.*

Dr. Raymond Costello
*Advisor For Equal Opportunities (Race) Liverpool Advisory Agency,
Liverpool City Council.*

Abdul Salam Gayle
*Development Officer - Liverpool Anti-Racist & Community Arts
Association (LARCAA).*

Garry Morris
*Out-reach Worker for the Trans-Atlantic Slavey Gallery
National Museums & Galleries on Merseyside.*

Donna Palmer
*Black Archives Researcher, Multi-Racial Library Promotion Unit,
Leisure Services Directorate Liverpool City Council.*

Ibrahim Thompson.
*Art Teacher employed by Liverpool Education Directorate, permanently attached
to Liverpool Anti-Racist & Community Arts Association.*

*" Until the lions have
their historians, tales of
hunting will always glorify
the hunter. "*
African proverb

*Back ground image: Kushites. Represented in a painting from a
royal tomb located in the Valley of The Kings, Egypt.*

'Slavery: An Introduction to The African Holocaust'

...with special reference to Liverpool..
"Capital of The Slave Trade."

Second Edition June 1997

ISBN 0 952478935

DISCLAIMER

DESIGN AND LAYOUT

*Race Equality Management Team
Liverpool Education Directorate*

PRINTING

Grosvenor Print, Bootle Liverpool.

FRONT COVER

*Detail of a slave head from frieze of
Liverpool Town Hall*

BACK COVER

*Background image: The Royal Liver Buildings at the Liverpool water front. Inset image: Detail from the Cunard Building {Custom House} adjacent to the Royal Liver Buildings.
Back inside page: African head from house entrance on Ullett Road, Liverpool.*

SLAVERY:
An Introduction To The African Holocaust
Revised edition June 1997

CONTENTS (Part One)

Background image: Charles Cordier. Negre en Costume Algerien - 1857.   Bronz, onyx and marble.

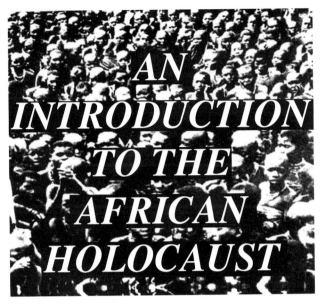

AN INTRODUCTION TO THE AFRICAN HOLOCAUST

The idea of producing a resource which would look, in depth, at the history of the African diaspora is certainly not new. The production of a history resource which would fit with the aims and objectives, attainment targets and skills of the National Curriculum for History has been done before. What is new about *'An Introduction To The African Holocaust'* relates to the perspective deployed by the Black History Resource Working Group (BHRWG). This perspective is inextricably linked to the experiences of the BHRWG members. When taken together they represent many years of research, of exposing racism and of developing strategies in order to combat racism.

Such a critical and challenging perspective has been put into operation throughout the book when collecting materials and presenting each of the sections; researching the experience of the African diaspora and when structuring exercises and activities for young people. We believe that, when taken as a whole, all sections of *'An Introduction To The African Holocaust'* give a more accurate insight into the enforced movement and dispersal of people from Africa.

The use of the word *'Holocaust'* in the title of the book was a decision over which there was some deliberation by group members. Group members wanted to use a word that would best describe the sheer horror, decimation of lives and magnitude of the slave trade. The word holocaust, we feel, sums this up. Most dictionary definitions for the word holocaust relate in some way to fire, for example, *"whole burnt offering", (1) "a sacrifice in which the whole of the victim was burnt"(2)* and *"destruction by fire"(3).* The Oxford English Dictionary (OED) 1989 (4) makes specific reference to particular groups at certain identifiable points in time. It gives as a definition for the term, *'The Holocaust': "..the mass murder of Jews by Nazis 1939-45"*. As stated, the essence of the word that the BHRWG wanted to capture was that which related to horror, mass murder and the decimation of a people. With this in mind, the dictionary definitions which we have associated the word 'holocaust' most closely with are, *"the total destruction of life"* (Harraps), *"wholesale sacrifice or destruction."* (Chambers).

The first syllable in the word holocaust, *"holo"* derives from the word whole and the second syllable, *"caust"*, or *"kaustos"* derives from the word burnt. Hence whole burnt. The word 'holocaust' is from Greek and Latin extraction and was used by Milton in 1671, and by Louis V11 in 1833.

The BHRWG was also of the opinion that language is dynamic and as such is subject to change and reinterpretation. Words are and should be used to apply to both new and old situations and historical events with which they are not traditionally associated.

If holocaust is taken to mean something horrific which has happened to a great many people then slavery was truly a holocaust. In terms of sheer numbers Professor Alkalimat *'Africa Before and After The Slave Trade'* (5) notes that there is considerable controversy about the impact of the slave trade in Africa, especially regarding the number of people exported from Africa. In fact estimates of the number of Africans taken to the Americas range from 100 million to a few million. Alkalimat continues:

> *"recent estimates of ten million tend to underestimate the extent of the slave trade. Just as the number of slaves exported from Africa is underestimated, so too are the mortality rates - the numbers of Africans who died on the voyage from Africa to the Americas. While some recent studies suggest that only 9 out of every 100 died, earlier studies show that the number of slaves who died was as high as 33 out of every 100! If we take into account the number of Africans who died in slave raids and of foreign diseases imported to Africa by slave*

traders, any estimates of the number of slaves imported to the Americas must be multiplied several times".*

All sections of the book explore in detail the true horrors of the slave trade in terms of, (sic) *"man's inhumanity to man" (6)* and the destruction of cultures and civilizations. The section on the 'Middle Passage' highlights the personal and collective holocaust of those who had the misfortune to be a part of it.

The need for a Black perspective to be applied to the history of Black people in Britain cannot be overstated. The current omission of such a perspective in history serves to explain, to some extent, why young Black people have little interest in conventional Eurocentric school history, a history which clearly tells them little about themselves and their ancestors. Furthermore, many white children and teachers have serious misconceptions about the history of Black people. Typically they know little of issues such as slavery, how Black people experienced it, why Europeans were involved in it, and why and how it ended.

Liverpool forms the focus for the book. This seems a particularly appropriate place to start given the central role that Liverpool played in the slave trade. To a large degree historians have failed to examine the full extent of the involvement of the city in the slave trade. In fact most local historians have been preoccupied with attempts to grapple with the problem of explaining why Liverpool continued to dominate British and European slave trading when it had become generally unacceptable to merchants in other parts of the country. Characteristically historians have played down Liverpool's involvement in slavery and have forgotten to even mention it in some 'complete' histories of the city. In contrast, the same historians have bolstered up the part played by local white abolitionists in the ending of the slave trade. As Cameron and Cooke (7) state of local historians:

"Their concern was not to explain the role of slavery, and the slave trade, in the development of capitalism. Such an approach was alien to their concept of history. Liverpool historians turned their attention in quite a different direction: that of rescuing the 'honour' of their native town."

Green (8) makes a similar point in relation to the presentation of history when he remarks that British historians have written about slavery, *"almost as if Britain had introduced Negro slavery solely for the satisfaction of abolishing it."*

We believe that a thorough and honest exploration of Liverpool's history is crucial to a true understanding of the slave trade and slavery. It is for this reason that the Black History Resource Working Group show how the enslavement of African people was *'normalised'*, how Members of Parliament, Lord Mayors (a Liberal Prime Minister), Bankers, the Clergy and other high ranking and well known individuals and families profited from slavery and how they were rewarded for their efforts. This reward came not only financially, but also in status and respect. Liverpool street names, monuments, districts and buildings stand as testament to this fact.

The Black History Resource Working Group was aware that the core study units for the National Curriculum for History are not supposed to be about issues such as the slave trade. But how would it be possible, for example, to teach children about sea-power and the extent of the British Empire (1750 - 1900), patterns of trade with the Empire, capital and the power of industry and religious diversity and social reform without a full consideration of the Black experience in this country and the colonies? All of these areas are identified as being essential within the framework of the National Curriculum for History.

A close reading of the book and following up on the suggested activities will mean that teachers will be able to realise the purpose of the Study Unit on *'Expansion, Trade And Industry'*, particularly in the context of worldwide expansion. The links of the book to units which proceed it, such as people of Victorian England in Key Stage Two, are clear. The final section of the resource pack links with the history of Britain in the 20th century.

'An Introduction To The African Holocaust' does not profess to cover all of the 'essential information' as highlighted in History Study Unit Three of the National Curriculum for History. In this sense it is as partial as any other school history resource. It is, however, more balanced than most in that it presents a detailed account of the African diaspora before, during and after slavery. It also presents Black people as resilient, never accepting their lot

passively, but rather rising up against slavery, colonisation and racism.

The Black History Resource Working Group anticipate that *'Slavery: An Introduction to The African Holocaust'* *will* be used with other resources in a complimentary manner.

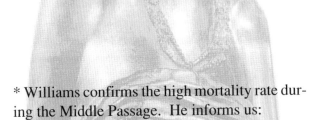

* Williams confirms the high mortality rate during the Middle Passage. He informs us:

"From the statistics kept by several vessels, it appears that out of 7904 slaves purchased on the coast, 2053 died on the middle passage. In one document, the average is put at 20 per cent., and in the case of the John, the mortality rate was actually 50 per cent." (10)

Throughout the book various figures are given for the number of people who were taken as slaves from Africa: there is no consensus of opinion. Irrespective of which number we use, what we must be clear on when discussing the issue with pupils, students and colleagues is the sheer magnitude.

Background image (left) Charles Cordier.
'Venus Africaine' - 1851
Detail: Francis Barber ('Study of a Black Man' - 1770) by Joshua Reynolds

4

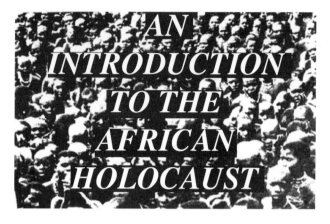

MAIN AIMS

A)   To show the link between historical events and the way in which contemporary society functions. This is particularly important when exploring the final section and looking at the way in which the ideologies used to justify the slave trade still have a bearing on the lives of people today.

B)   To enable pupils and students to understand that history is not an absolute objective study. They should be aware that it is largely about interpretation and that the interests of the *'tellers of history'* are often at work when presenting information or evidence to support a particular stance. A thorough evaluation of the evidence and of the motivations of writers will enable students to give informed opinions based on analyses.

C)   To enable pupils and students to examine evidence critically. This will facilitate their arrival at answers and conclusions which can be supported by reliable information.

D)   To facilitate the development of curiosity, questioning, self-awareness and self-esteem.

E)   To enable students to examine a number of ideas and concepts such as power, change, continuity, industrialisation, under-development, resistance and racism.

The Black History Resource Working Group is committed to networking with teachers and educationalists around the production of resources which reflect the fact that Britain is a multiracial society. As such we welcome feedback, and discussion on any aspect of this, past and future curriculum resources.

A LOCAL PERSPECTIVE

Although *'An Introduction To The African Holocaust'* focuses on the city of Liverpool, this does not mean it only has relevance to local educa-

tors, pupils and students. Through local studies in different regions, working with Black comunities, local museums and exploring various archive materials similar resources to those retrieved in Liverpool can be utilised.

It remains the case however, that the type of information will vary given that regional histories often do. Liverpool as the focus for slavery takes on a particular significance given the documented evidence which places it so firmly at the centre of the slave trade from the early 1700s up until the abolition of the slave trade in 1807. Further, the experiences of so many generations of Black people in Liverpool means that the book has a local immediacy. The exercises, activities and resources which are presented as part of this publication have been designed in such a way as to have national applicability. They are meant to engender a critical evaluation and awareness of information being presented.

HOW SHOULD THE BOOK BE USED?

The book has been arranged in two distinct parts, the first of which contains detailed notes for teachers and educationalists. Each section of Part One contains detailed information in relation to the subject area. It is hoped that teachers will reproduce this information in precis form for younger pupils and present it as it is for older students. Questions and exercises can then be devised in relation to this information and used in conjunction with the practical suggestions given in Part Two.

After giving some information on each of the sections, details are given about how the information meets with the requirements of the National Curriculum for History. These activities are general and tend to emphasis the skills that pupils and students should acquire or further develop through the completion of exercises, activities, research and reading.

In addition to this, learning outcomes are detailed as well as the main aims of each of the sections. Where possible the main skills as outlined in the history curriculum are given. Further, there has been a full consideration of the new History draft proposals (9) (for consultation until 29th July

1994) as well as the final Curriculum Orders (December 1994) and regulations for history when detailing how each section fits with National Curriculum requirements.

In accordance with the new proposals it is made clear that the history curriculum must take the lead in: *"ensuring a predominant emphasis on British history"*. The Black History Resource Working Group is of the opinion that a full consideration of slavery would be in keeping with this for it was during the period from 1750 - 1900 that Britain and Europe had a significant impact on the under development of African societies. Further the Group is of the opinion that the book fits within the main statement in relation to the purpose of Core Study Unit Three as stated in the history Draft Proposals thus:

"Pupils should be taught to understand how developments from the early Middle Ages to the twentieth century helped shape the economy, society, culture and political structures of modern Britain. They should have opportunities to study developments in Europe and the non-European world, and, drawing on their awareness of chronology, to make links and connections between historical events and developments in the different periods and areas studied. They should be given opportunities to use their historical knowledge to evaluate and use sources of information, and to construct accounts and explanations of historical events and developments".

To accompany each section in Part One there are exercises and activities in Part Two. The Black History Resource Working Group have devised exercises and activities in a varied manner to test and help develop certain skills. Through the exercises and activities pupils and students should be encouraged to challenge their own preconceptions, engender a critical awareness and improve their powers of analysis, deduction and empathy.

For both parts of the book there is a full bibliography and details of sources. This information should be used to encourage pupils and students to get involved in follow-up work. There are a number of suggestions given in Part Two

of how pupils and students can get involved in finding out information for themselves.

The Black History Resource Working Group has tried to cover the main areas in the history of the Africa diaspora as they relate to slavery, but through necessity and given practical considerations, for example the availability of resources and materials, some sections are more detailed than others. In the future the group will endeavour to explore all sections further through continued research. For the moment we hope that *'Slavery: An Introduction to The African Holocaust'* can serve as a first step towards providing a true and honest resource which will help to facilitate access to one aspect of the history of the African diaspora.

***The Black History Resource Working Group
March 1995 (Revised June 1997)***

*Image: Marie-Guilhelmine Benoist.
'Portrait D'Une Negress'. 1800*

REFERENCES

(1) *Chambers Dictionary* 1986 Edition.

(2) *Harraps Dictionary* 1988 Edition.

(3) *Oxford English Dictionary* (Illustrated) 1990.

(4) *Oxford English Dictionary* 1989. Oxford University Press.

(5) **Professor Alkalimat** *'Africa Before And After The Slave Trade'*. Published by 21st Century Books. 6th Edition 1986

(6) **Dicky Sam** *'Liverpool And Slavery'*. Centenary Edition. Published by Scouse Press. First published in 1894.

(7) **G. Cameron & S.Cooke** *Liverpool Capital Of The Slave Trade'*. Published by Picton Press 1992

(8) **W.A.Green** *'British Slave Emancipation: The Sugar Colonies And The Great Experiment 1830-65'*. Quoted in: *'Black People In The British Empire: An Introduction'* **Peter Fryer,** Pluto Press 1988.

(9) *Draft Proposal Document for the National Curriculum for History* - July 1994.

(10) **Gomer Williams** - *'Liverpool Slavers And Privateers - With An Account of The Liverpool Slave Trade'*. Published by Heinemann 1897 and 1966.

Background image: Eugene Delacroix - 'Head of a Black Wearing a Turban'. Pastel on paper

SLAVERY THROUGH THE AGES

The aim of this section is to examine the history of slavery through the ages to understand how it was perpetuated and maintained. The section also deals with African slavery and its transformation into a capitalist enterprise which was used to develop the economies of Europe and the United States of America.

INTRODUCTION

" There have been slaves (rightless person/wageless labour) in many different parts of the world, and in many different times in history. Slaves are men and women who are somebody else's property, their owner can buy and sell them just like any other object." (1)

Slavery began in prehistoric times reaching its peak in Ancient Greece and the Roman Empire. During the Middle Ages slavery declined. With the colonization of the 'New World' during the 1500 and 1600s by Europeans, there was a great demand for slaves.

THE BACKGROUND

It has been said that the start of slavery probably followed the development of farming about 10,000 years ago. Farming gave people the opportunity to put their prisoners of war to work.

"Slaves came from many different sources, the most frequent was capture in war. Others were kidnapped on slave-raiding or piracy expeditions. Many slaves were the offspring of slaves. Some people were enslaved as a punishment for crime or debt, others were sold into slavery by their parents, other relatives or even spouses... Another source of slavery was self-sale, undertaken sometimes to obtain an elite position, sometimes to escape destitution." (2)

It must be understood that for slavery to flourish, social status and social class are essential. Also essential is an economic surplus. Slaves were often consumption goods who themselves had to be maintained rather than productive assets who generated income for their owner. In *'Discovering Africa's Past'* Basil Davidson explains that prior to the trans-Atlantic slave trade:

" they (slaves) were well cared for because they were expensive. Only the rich could afford them." (3)

Owners expected economic gain from slave owner-ship:

"Free land and open resources were often needed before a slave system could be established. Slavery expanded as commerce and industry increased, the growth of trade created a demand for a disciplined labour force that could produce goods for export." Davidson (ibid).

There were two types of slaves. Firstly, household/domestic slaves. Domestic slaves occasionally worked outside the house, for example in haying or harvesting. Secondly, productive slaves were kept predominantly to produce marketable commodities in mines and plantations.

ANCIENT TIMES

Slavery, existed throughout Asia, including China and the Indian Sub-Continent. In China slavery existed in the Shang dynasty, 18-12th centuries BC. In ancient Han China (206 BC-AD 25), five per cent of the population was enslaved.

In Korea there was a large number of slaves, ranging from a third to a half of the entire population, for most of the millennium between the Silla period and the mid 18th century.

Slavery existed in ancient India where it is recorded in Sanskrit Laws of the Manu of the first century BC. In 1841 it was estimated that there were between 8 and 9 million slaves in India.

Slavery was widely practised in other Asian countries including , Burma, Thailand, Philippines, Nepal, Malay, Indonesia, Japan and parts of Eastern Europe.

Slavery was very much in evidence in the Middle East from the beginning of recorded history. It was treated as a prominent institution in the Babylonian Code of Hamurabi 1750 BC

Slaves were present in Ancient Egypt, Greece and Rome and are also mentioned prominently in the Bible among the Hebrews in Palestine.

In ancient times slavery reached its fullest development in the empires of Greece and Rome. Slaves did most of the work in these societies in the mines and plantations. Others did household work and some even became professionals such as doctors and writers. During the period of 400 BC slaves may have made up about one third of the population of Athens. In Rome, slavery became so widespread that even common people owned slaves. Most people of the ancient world regarded slavery as a natural condition that could befall anyone at any time. The treatment of slaves varied greatly, but almost all slaves could legally marry, have a family, testify in court or own property.

In ancient Greece and the Roman Empire, slaves who worked in large gangs in mines or on plantations served long hours and suffered harsh punishment. Those who worked as household servants were treated as well as any member or their owner's family.

A slave's hope was **manumission**, which was formal release from slavery by the owner. Most ancient slave owning societies allowed manumission. Slavery was also a feature of European society; slaves were prominent in Scandinavia during the Viking era, AD 800-1050 and after.

MIDDLE AGES

Throughout most of Europe household slavery went on well into the late Middle Ages and gradually changed into serfdom, after the break-up of the Roman Empire. At this time cAD 400s trade fell sharply and there was the loss of markets for goods that slaves might have produced which led to the decline in the need for slaves.

Slavery continued in the areas around the Mediterranean Sea. Most of this resulted from fighting between the Christians and Muslims. Between AD 600 and 700, the Arab Muslims conquered the Middle East and North Africa, and almost all of Spain. Christians and Muslims fought each other for hundreds of years, and both groups enslaved each other's prisoners. *"....Christians like Muslims, saw nothing wrong about enslaving non-believers." Davidson (ibid).*

Continental Europe, France, Germany, Spain, Italy and Portugal all had slavery. In England about ten per cent of the population entered the Domesday Book in 1086 were slaves.

By the end of the Middle Ages slavery no longer existed in England and the famous Cartwright decision of the reign of Elizabeth I (1569) held that, *"England was too pure an air for slaves to breathe in." (4)* Slavic slaves were plentiful in the Italian states as late as the 14th century,

> *"Christian states, especially the city-states of Italy such as Genoa and Venice, sold large numbers of European slaves to the king of Egypt and western Asia". Davidson (ibid).*

Euorpean slaves mainly came from countries of eastern Europe, they were considered to be 'non-believers', as the Slavic countries converted to Christianity later than the rest of Europe.

> *"The word slave comes from Slav, Slavs are people who live mainly in eastern and central Europe. Russians, Bulgarians, Poles, Czech, Slovaks and Serbs are all Slavonic people. They speak languages which are similar to one another and have developed from the same root. Slavs were often taken prisoners and enslaved, first by German Knights in the Early Middle Ages and later by Ottoman Turks." Oxford Children's Dictionary (ibid).*

These were soon to be replaced by African slaves on the sugar plantations of several Mediterranean Islands.

In 1441 ten (African) slaves had already been sent to Portugal by the explorer Gonzalves, and were presented to Prince Henry of Portugal who hoped to convert them to Christianity and subsequently send them back to their countries as missionaries; this did not happen and more slaves were sent to Portugal. By the time of Prince Henry's death in 1460 between 700 and 800 slaves were being exported annually to Portugal.

Prince Henry was said to have condemned the sale of slaves, but his successors actively participated in it. It is alleged that between 1486 and 1495 an average of 448 slaves belonging to the Portuguese crown were imported annually into Portugal. The export of slaves was not confined to Portugal or even to the Iberian Peninsular; but escalated and extended across the Atlantic to the Americas.

When the Spaniards began to explore North and South America between 1492 and 1504 establishing plantations and exploiting the natural resources, problems arose because of the unsuitability of the indigenous people.

As such the Portuguese who were already used to African slave labour found the export of Africans to the newly encountered lands of America a solution to the problem.

"The first batch of slaves exported to the Americas in 1501 came from Lisbon in Portugal, and from then on more slaves came from Lisbon. This state of affairs continued for almost 20 years till the first direct transportation from the West Coast of Africa was effected in 1521. As more mines opened up and more plantations were set up, the demand for slaves increased. Between 1530 and 1600 an average of 13,000 slaves per annum were being exported to the Americas. The number rose to about 27,500 a year by 17th century; 70,000 in the 18th century and by the 1830's the number had increased to 135,000 per annum". Phillott (5).

There are no decisive agreements about the number of people who were captured and exported as slaves from Africa. The debate goes on: for example in *'Slavery and African Life'* Patrick Manning (6) says,

"As a cumulative total, some 14 million persons were exported from tropical Africa as slaves in the eighteenth and nineteenth centuries: 9 million from the West-

ern Coast, 3 million from the Savanna and Horn, and 2 million from the Eastern Coast. In the sixteenth and seventeenth centuries the Western Coast had exported 2 million, and the Savanna and Horn had exported another 2 million, so that the grand total of slaves exported from Africa since 1500 is roughly 18 million."

In *'A Peoples History of the United States'* (7) Howard Zinn introduces another dimension into the argument. He describes the numbers of people who were not only captured but also those who died on the voyage as a much higher figure:

"By 1800 nearly 15 million Africans had been brought to the new world. Another 50 million black people are estimated to have died en route or soon after arrival. When Europe finally gave up slavery at the end of the eighteenth century, one in four Africans were slaves."

THE AFRICAN SLAVE TRADE

Slavery in Africa was not a new phenomenon: it had existed in some form for many centuries before the period of 'Modern Slavery' from the mid 1400s. Most African communities had slaves, although the way they were treated and the kind of work they did varied greatly from one society to another.

In some African societies slaves from other African states were highly regarded for their loyalty. They often became soldiers and senior officials.

"Prisoners of war and convicted criminals were often treated as 'wageless labour', liable to be bought and sold. They were not chattels as they came to be in the mines and plantations of the Americas." (Davidson ibid).

In African societies there were no clear and rigid divisions between the bonded and the free. Everyone was a working member of a domestic group, attached normally through kinship. Slaves were working members of a group but since they were not kin their status was lower.

Slaves could advance through work; they could buy their freedom with the produce of the plot of land assigned to them for cultivation. A slave could advance through good fortune by inheriting goods or marrying his master's daughter. It was not unusual for slaves to acquire positions of great influence and power. This system was not only unique to the African slave system Davidson in *'Discovering Africa's Past'* explains,

"As in Africa they (European slaves) became 'rightless persons' who could be bought and sold, or given as gifts, to serve as domestic staff or skilled craftsmen. They could rise to positions of authority, marry into their masters' families, work themselves to freedom."

As a rule slaves did much of the back-breaking work of agriculture. In the West African Kingdom of Asante thousands of slaves were employed in the gold mines.

People writing about the trans-Atlantic slave trade at that period in history such as Olaudah Equiano argued that compared to plantation slavery in the Americas, the lot of a slave in Africa was relatively free and easy.

There is no conclusive agreement as to why the African aristocracies co-operated with the Europeans in selling their captives into slavery. One explanation could be that it was the surplus of captive labour within African society that established the means of overseas slavery. African chiefs and kings sold their slaves to Europeans just as they had always sold them to one another. In the period before 1750 few Africans or Europeans thought anything was wrong with buying, selling and owning human beings.

Nine years after Columbus' first trip across the Atlantic, the Spanish throne issued a proclamation legalizing the importation of slaves to the Americas. Not long after that the African slave trade was transformed into a major commercial enterprise.

Methods of enslavement varied, but there were four main ways in which a person could be enslaved: criminals were sold by chiefs as punishment; free Africans were obtained from slave raids; domestic slaves were sold and prisoners of war were enslaved.

The slaves were bartered for European goods such as guns and gunpowder, cloth, rum, beads, iron and copper bars. As trading became more established the price of individual slaves bought in Africa rose from £10 at the beginning of the eighteenth century to £27 by the end.

As with the numbers of Africans who were exported, there is also debate about the role of the African aristocracies in the capture and export of slaves.

African scholars and even politicians now acknowledge that the enslavement and sale of Africans was initially supported by the Africans themselves, especially the coastal kings and their elders. However, and as we have shown, African slavery did differ from chattel slavery, and there were, even in the 17th century, many opponents to it.

There were African rulers like King Nzinga Mvemba of Kongo who attempted to stop the taking of slaves from his state. He met bitter opposition and several attempts were made on his life.

Out of the grim but profitable business of the slave trade new political units came into being. The city-states of the Niger delta, which were only small fishing villages, prospered and formed themselves into a highly organised trading network based on the export of men and women. As late as the 1820's, 20,000 people a year were being shipped out from the Niger delta states and traded to Europeans.

In the early years slave trading resulted in economic prosperity for the coast states of Africa. But the older inland communities suffered the loss of both wealth and population as the desire for European manufactured items became dependent upon a never ending supply of captives, forcing states into continual acts of aggression and violence against one another. After 1700 slave raiding was carried out with European fire-arms.

Many communities were persecuted and destroyed, others fled their ancestral homelands to avoid the slave raiders. The local population never gained any long term benefit from slavery.

"....the slave trade did not confer benefits of any kind on West Africa. On the contrary, it was an unmitigated misery, ... It led in the first place to an unpardonable destruction of population. During the whole period of the trade, it has been estimated

that between 30 and 40 million souls were lost to Africa, the victims were often the most virile men and women. The raiding which the trade generated and steadily intensified caused a great deal of misery, bloodshed, destruction as whole towns and villages were burnt down and as many people killed as were caught." Davidson (ibid)

Slavery gave the Europeans a foothold in Africa and thereby prepared the way for the European colonial invasion with the partition of Africa in the late nineteenth century. The slave trade went on for 400 years. The continent has never recovered from the effects of the slave trade which has affected its history and determined its present economic situation.

LEARNING OUTCOMES

a) Pupils and students will be aware of the fact that there have been different types of slavery historically and that modern slavery, that is since the mid 1400s, differs significantly from anything which preceeded it. They will be aware of the fact that slavery has existed for approximately 10, 000 years.

b) Pupils and students will be aware that there was slavery in Africa prior to the arrival of Europeans, but know that the slavery which existed there was significantly different from what come to be known as 'Chattel slavery'. It is important that young people understand that in African societies it was possible for slaves to buy, or acquire their freedom, marry into the tribes which enslaved them and be treated with respect and recognised for their skills.

c) Pupils and students should know that African tribal leaders sold slaves to Europeans, but that they had little or no conception as to what might happen to those people. Further to this it is important to make them aware of the fact that Europeans encouraged African leaders to sell slaves through a variety of economic incentives.

d) Pupils and students will be aware that Europeans exploited tribal divisions through the introduction of guns. This served their aims as it made it possible for the capture of increasingly large numbers of Africans as the slave trade reached its zenith.

e) Chattel slavery is a particularly brutal form of slavery characteristic of the modern European slavery from the 15th - 18th century. Pupils and students should be aware that the European involvement in slavery was economically orientated. It was primarily about the forced movement of Africans to the Americas. Africans were the hub of the process of production; it was their labour which produced the raw materials to be traded in Europe. This in turn generated income for traders who were able to finance voyages to Africa with goods to trade with local chiefs, and so the process was self generating.

NATIONAL CURRICULUM

A) Pupils and students will be able to explain the differences between modern slavery and the types of slavery which preceded it. This will involve them in examining primary and secondary resource materials and extracting relevant information.

B) Through examining relevant materials pupils and students will be in a position to make judgements about the reliability of historical sources by reference to the circumstances in which they were produced.

C) Through a close reading of suggested written materials pupils and students will be aware of the various features of different societies in history. Specifically within this section, African and European societies.

D) Pupils and students will become familiar with certain concepts and terminology, both in relation to the passage of time and to various types of slavery and societies.

E) Pupils and students will be given the opportunity to draw information from a range of historical sources including: contemporary accounts; pictures and illustrations; charts tables and various texts.

F) Pupils and students will be able to relate the colonisation of various African countries and islands in the 'New World', to the economic expansion of Europe and Britain in particular.

G) Pupils and students will understand basic economic principles in relation to production, agriculture, labour, profit, investment and trade. They will also be aware that the success of modern slavery depended on the exploitation of African labour and securing colonies in the Americas.

REFERENCES

(1) **M.Worrall** (ed) *'Oxford Children's Encyclopaedia'* Oxford University Press 1991.

(2) *'Encyclopaedia Britannica* 'Vol. 27 15th, Edition - 1994.

(3) **Basil Davidson** *'Discovering Africa's Past'* Published by Longman 1978.

(4) **Basil Davidson.** *'African Kingdoms'* Published by Time Inc. 1967.

(5) **Ruben Phillott** *'Black Studies: Notes on African- History' (out* of print) Published by Tube 1982.

(6) **Patrick Manning** *'Slavery and African Life. 'Cambridge* University Press 1990.

(7) **Howard Zinn** *'A People's History of The United States'* Harper & Row 1980.

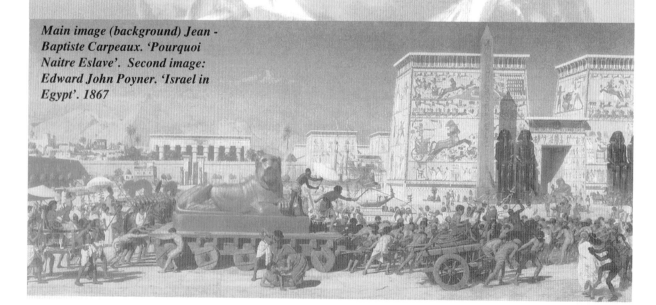

Main image (background) Jean - Baptiste Carpeaux. 'Pourquoi Naitre Eslave'. Second image: Edward John Poyner. 'Israel in Egypt'. 1867

AFRICA THE BIRTHPLACE OF MANKIND

The aim of this section is to look at Africa before the European slave trade disrupted its customs and cultures. There have been many European writers on African society and one of the most respected is Basil Davidson. He says of African society,

"They have created culture and civilizations, evolved systems of government and systems of thought, and pursued the inner life of the spirit with a consuming passion that has produced some of the finest art known to man." (1)

Some of the better known works of art are the Benin Bronze from West Africa, but lesser known works are cave paintings of African Stone Age life. Many examples of these are found in caves of the Sahara. From evidence found of fossil skulls and bones of 'homo sapiens', it is generally agreed that mankind began in Africa. The oldest skeletons that can be identified as those of early man have been found in the Sudan and in the equatorial forests of the southern fringe of the Sahara. The earliest remains of man, homo sapiens, were found in Tanzania, East Africa. These date from 1.75 million years ago.

It is agreed that the ancestors of Africans had been on the continent longer than the Europeans in Europe, the Amerindians in the Americas or the Chinese in China. Africa had thriving societies with the emergence of cultural diversity seeing the development of more than a thousand different languages, different systems of behaviour and beliefs.

".....some of these systems produced societies whose standard of living in terms of food, personal safety and freedom,

equalled that of contemporary societies in Europe. In some instances they were even more advanced." Davidson (ibid).

Early merchants found prosperous, self-contained cities such as Timbuktu linked to one another by busy and carefully ordered trading system. They also found astute businessmen operating in a political and social system of varied flexibility and sophistication. For example, African societies practised a simple but effective form of social welfare within the tribal system in their concern for widows and orphaned children.

".... A tribe is not so much a racial unit but a social one, usually occupying a territory with recognised boundaries. It forms a closely knit, exclusive community bound by rules that are broken only on pain of death or banishment. The tribesmen share a tradition of descent from a common ancestor, a folklore, and a set of customs and behavioural patterns that have the force of law. Tribe members acknowledge a common system of government and unite for defence or aggression.... The tribe provided a complete cradle to the grave system of social security. Orphans, widows and the old were taken care of, and no-one went hungry except when all did in famine times." Encyclopaedia Britannica. (2).

KINGDOMS OF AFRICA

In this section we will be looking at the Kingdom of the Kushites and the Kindom of Ghana. They are only two of the great kingdoms of ancient Africa.

KUSH AND MEROITIC CIVILIZATIONS

Kush is the name that was given by the ancient Egyptians to the kingdoms which lay south of their borders. The kingdom became important in the time of the Meroitic people, and was the most ancient of the independent kingdoms of Africa. It was spread over a part of the country which is now known as Sudan, to the south of Egypt. Like Egypt, it has always been dependent on the river Nile for its life. From 2000 BC the history of Kush was closely linked with that of Egypt. About 1100 BC the Egyptian Empire began to decay and Kashta, king of the Kushites made his empire independent of Egypt and actually conquered its former masters by invasion. The Kushites ruled over Egypt as far north as Thebes, the capital of Upper Egypt. This happened about 700 BC, not very long after Kashta's son, Piankhy, completed the conquest of Egypt, and became ruler of a land which stretched from the shores of the Mediterranean to the borders of modern Ethiopia; almost a quarter of the African continent.

The capital of the Kushite kingdom was called Meroe, which stood on a crossing point of the river Nile for the caravans which carried trade east and west. Their route followed the Atabara into the Abyssinian hills and the Indian Ocean. Meroe was a centre of iron working; iron as a metal was increasing in importance at the time.

The period around the start of the Christian era is one of the peaks of Meroitic civilization, during this period many grand buildings were erected, tombs which have been excavated were found with magnificent elaborate jewels and glassware and bronze. At the temple of Isis were found many rich gifts which were sent regularly to the sanctuary of the goddess.

Kush was a highly wealthy and developed society with its own writing known as 'Meroitic cursive' writing - hieroglyphic. These hieroglyphics were similar to the Egyptian but differed in their value. They are written and read the opposite way around to Egyptian hieroglyphics; it has been said that this was a done in an attempt to be different. With these hieroglyphics there goes a cursive form of writing often abbreviated; the signs seem to be derived in part from the demotic writing used in Egypt at that period for administrative and private documents.

Very little is known about the language of the Kushites. In their alphabet there were twenty three signs used to represent the consonants, some vowels; and a syllabic group of 'colons' usually separates the individual words .

The Kushites and their great city of Meroe was well known in the ancient world. In the Bible, the Acts of the Apostles, we read of a Kushite (or Ethiopian as they were often called) who was converted to Christianity.

The Romans were intrigued by the Kushites and their country. Nero sent two centurions up

the River Nile; on their return they stated that the land was too poor to be worth conquering. Very little is known of the last centuries of the Kushites, but from excavations of burial places at Meroe, their graves were becoming poorer and less well built, and the grave goods fewer and less valuable. It would appear that Meroe grew gradually poorer, and probably did not continue to keep contact with its more prosperous countries to the north. Another contributory factor for the decline of the Kushites could have been tribal warfare.

The Axumite people from the southern tip of Arabia made a kingdom on the western coast of the Red Sea, the Kingdom of Axum. As the kingdom and power of the Kushites waned, the Axumite kingdom was becoming more important and probably annexed much of Meroe's trade. It is thought that by AD 350, there was a skirmish with the Axumites and the Kushites were conquered, their cities were burnt and destroyed. It has been suggested that the Kushites who fled possibly settled in the area around Lake Chad.

The Kushites were an African people, as were the Egyptians. Their close links with Egypt made them assume an Egyptian style in many things. This is evident if we look at their statues and paintings. The Kushites achieved a position of power and importance and won the respect of the civilized world as it was at that time.

GHANA

In this section we will only be looking at the state of Ghana, although other West African Empires were equal in greatness and power. Ghana was one of the Medieval States of West Africa, the others being Mali and Songhai and Kanem-Bornu

"each one.... seemed well advanced in matters of government and economic prosperity,.....each played an important part in the development of West Africa. Each rose to power in turn, and became a vital link in the commercial world of North Africa, which in its turn affected events in Europe - various countries were dependent on their import of Ghana gold through Africa for the stability of their currencies...." (3)

Ghana (AD 700-1200), Mali (1200-1500), Songhai (1350-1600) and Kanem-Bornu (800-1800) did not have fixed boundaries in the modern sense, but the area of West Africa was populated by groups of people whom for a time became the most powerful in a particular area. The most powerful groups would demand taxes, conscript men in times of war, or levy supplies of grain from the people who were settled as cultivators round about, but they had to be a strong group to enforce their demands. As their influence increased, more land and people came under their control, the rulers would appoint officers to collect the taxes and ensure order was kept.

> *"....The rulers claimed territory as their own but were not rulers in the modern sense; they left the people to govern themselves in their own way, but expected obedience and a ready response to their demands...." Shinnie (ibid)*

The ancient state of Ghana was a 1000 miles north of modern Ghana. Ghana was the first of the three states to rise to power. It is estimated that Ghana had been a power in West Africa since the Romans left North Africa in the fourth century AD.

As Ghana has an oral tradition much of its early written information and history is dependent on writers who came into contact with its people.

> *"One writer, El Zuhri, tells us that the people of Ghana attacked neighbours, 'who knew not iron and fight with bars of ebony'. The Ghanians 'defeat them because they fight with swords and lances'." Shinnie (ibid).*

From about AD 734 Ghana was known as "the land of gold". The Arabs were interested in capturing the source of the gold for which Ghana was famous. To the north of the land controlled by Ghana and south of the Atlas mountains was the meeting point for Arab and African trade at a town called Sijilmasa. Here the Soninke of Ghana sent their gold to exchange for goods that they wanted, and particularly for salt, of which there were no supplies further south. The salt was then taken south, and exchanged for gold, as the Soninke were not gold miners. The gold was mined by people in a district called Wangar, which lay outside the political control of Ghana. The Soninke acted as middlemen between the gold producers and the Arabs who wanted to acquire the gold. The Arabs in turn sold or traded the gold with the Europeans.

African markets were the main sources of gold before the 'discovery' of America. Europe, and European states depended on 'Guinea gold' for financial enterprises.

The Wangara people had a great appetite for salt as they had no supply in their own country. Many products such as copper, cloth, dried fruit and cowrie shells were also accepted in the exchange for gold. It was salt the miners really wanted, so much so, it was said that they gave gold in equal weight to the salt they received!

In regulating the supply of gold, Ghana imposed taxes on every load of goods which entered or left the area over which it had political control. The gold trade was highly organised; it was on this that the wealth and importance of Ghana was based. We are told that Ghana was a great power having a formidable army, the king being able to put together two hundred thousand warriors armed with bows and arrows, iron weapons, swords and daggers. The state of Ghana was very prosperous and wealthy but was unable to develop and grow in peace. There were continual quarrels and fighting between the Soninke and some of their stronger neighbours, the Lemtuna and the Jedala who lived to the north of Ghana. The Lemtuna captured from Ghana the town of Audoghast, which had been a tax paying city, and a place of some importance.

In turn, another group of people, the Almoravids from north Africa, set out on a holy war to convert the people of Audoghast to Islam and captured the town from the Lemtuna, about AD 1054.

The Almoravids were powerful and attacked Ghana. The Soninke were strong enough to keep them at bay for some time, and the capital Kumbi Saleh of Ghana did not fall until AD 1076. In 1087 Ghana regained its independence from the Almoravids; however the years under Almoravid rule had weakened Ghana's links with the people it controlled and authority over them was lost. Some people split off and became separate kingdoms pledging no allegiance to Ghana. The empire of Ghana shrank and never recovered. By AD 1203 Ghana was in ruins. The neighbouring Sossos captured it and reduced its inhabitants to slavery. In 1235 the Sossos were defeated by the Mandingo and Ghana finaly became part of the Mali Empire.

SOUTH AMERICAN CIVILIZATIONS

Introduction

The native peoples of the Americas and the Caribbean islands are known as Amerindian. Their story began in pre-historic times long before written records.

It is thought that hunters first entered America over 50,000 years ago following animals across the ice from Asia to Alaska. In a publication entitled *'A History of the Aztecs and the Mayas and their Conquest'* (4), Alfred Sundel says,

" The conservative view is that separate bands of wanders trudged from Siberia to Alaska across the Bering Straits by way of a frozen bridge of pack ice or a stretch of land raised by the sunken sea level. Several migrations along this avenue are believed to have come out of Asia over the course of thirty thousand years."

As more people crossed the bridge other groups of hunters followed pushing those who came before further south. Once the peoples of the Americas and the Caribbean Islands had become settled on the land, from about 7000 BC they began cultivation as a means of survival.

By 5000 BC the peoples on the American continent were enjoying a varied diet of maize, morrow and chilli. The people on the Caribbean Islands were not only cultivating staple foods such as yams, cassava, and cacao but also tobacco which the Arawaks had been producing for centuries.

"Tobacco is the only native crop which became an important article of export from the West Indies after European occupation." (Parry and Sherlock 5) .

Agriculture in the Americas was very successful, enabling the Mayas in Central America, the Aztecs in Mexico and the Incas in Peru to produce surplus. This surplus was not only for eating but also storage, trade and exchange for other goods and for paying taxes.

"the food surplus made it possible for the numbers of Aztecs, Incas and Mayas to increase and for their societies to become very complex, and divided into people of different groups and occupations..." (6)

These societies became stratified with kings, nobles and warriors who conquered neighbouring peoples creating large empires. Towns and cities grew, builders, artisans, craftsmen, weavers and artist emerged. At the bottom of the society were the common people who toiled in the fields or worked on the building sites, making magnificent stone cities, bridges, aqueducts and roads which were typical of the Maya, Aztec and Inca civilizations.

THE MAYAS

The Mayas ruled over a vast area of Central America which includes modern Mexico. During the 4th - 10th centuries AD they had built and developed one of the most remarakable civilizations

"The Mayas lived in many independent city-states... In each was a hereditary 'priest-king' who ruled the countryside around its central temple-city with the aid of priests and nobles." Hall (ibid).

The Mayas were skilled at mathematics, astronomy and astrology. They used hieroglyphs and drawings to record their history, ideas and beliefs. Towards the end of the 12th century the Mayan empire rapidly declined, due to a growing division between the ruling priests and common folk.

THE AZTECS

The Aztecs also ruled over a vast area of South America. Their empire stretched across from modern Guatemala in the south, to Texas in the north. The Aztecs were governed by an emporer who was assisted by nobles. The emperor had two important functions the first was ruler of the empire and the second was to serve as high priest in the Aztec religion. The Aztecs were famous as warriors and traders, and enjoyed a full cultural life of poetry, dancing, organised games and ceremonies. They built magnificent temples and palaces.

THE INCAS

The Inca Empire covered almost the entire area of South America west of the Andes, from Ecuador to northern Chile, and spreading eastwards over the high ranges to the borders of the Amazonian and Bolivian forest. The Empire was governed by a god-king, known as the Lord Inca. The Incas were gifted civil and military engineers and administrators. They kept records and accounts on the **quipu**, a device of strings of beads of different shapes, sizes and colours (which they put in different arrangements). The land over which the Incas ruled was rich in gold and silver, and they were skilled craftsmen in the working of these metals.

PEOPLES OF THE CARIBBEAN

The earliest known settlers on the Caribbean Island were the Siboney Indians who were thought to have arrived from the Florida peninsula. Very little is known about the Siboney, but it is thought that they were hunter gathers. Two thousand years ago other Amerindians travelled to the Caribbean Islands: the Arawaks, who were followed by the Caribs.

They originally lived in South America, in what is now known as Venezuela and Guyana. No one knows why these people left the mainland but it has been suggested that it may have been because the Caribbean Islands had less dense jungle, a fresher climate and no dangerous animals. It has been suggested that the Caribs were warriors, unlike the peaceful Arawaks, who probably saw the Islands as a place of safety from the Caribs.

Very little is known about the Caribbean Islands before the arrival of the Spaniards, but what we do know is that they renamed the majority of them. For example the Island of Guanahani was renamed San Salvador.

One name that we are certain has remained in more or less its original form is that of the island of Jamaica, the modern spelling, or 'Yameque' as it was originally pronounced. There is also doubt about the name of the Caribbean region. It is thought that the name was given by the Spanish and derives from the word 'Canib' or Carib, people who eat humans. It has been said by Claypole (7)

"... the Arawaks occupied all the greater islands of the Caribbean; but in the easternmost island, Puerto Rico, they were already suffering from raids of an intrusive and far more warlike people, to whom the Spaniards gave the name Caribs. Caribs means cannibal."

In a book published in 1992 by Peter Hulme and Neil Whitehead, *'Wild Majesty'* (8) a new insight is given into the history of the Caribs. This shows that more research and investigation is needed in order to gain an accurate insight into the lives of both the Caribs and the Arawaks.

"There are many questions the book does not address, most notably the whole problem of the definition and use of the word 'Carib' in the fifteenth the subsequent centuries. For many years, indeed for many centuries, outsiders have imposed a cultural schema on the native Caribbean, separating the 'peaceful' Arawaks of the larger islands to the west and north from the 'fierce' in fact 'cannibalistic', Caribs of the south and east. 'Carib' or some variant such as 'Caniba' was taken as so clearly synonymous with the practice of men-eating that the word 'cannibalism' (and its cognates) replaced 'anthropophagy' in most European languages."

The idea of fierce Caribs chasing timid Arawaks from one Caribbean island to another is being contested by many historians; for it represent too simplistic a picture of life in the islands prior to the arrival of the Europeans.

THE ARAWAKS

The Arawaks were farmers , who grew subsistence crops and tobacco. Hunting, fishing and gathering wild fruits formed a part of their daily activities.

As they were a peaceful nation their only weapons were spears and clubs. Most long journeys were made on foot or by boat as they had no riding animals or beasts of burden. They built canoes from cotton trees, which varied in size. The largest could take seventy or eighty men.

Entertainment was varied,consisting of sports like running, wrestling and ball games. The balls were made from the gum tree and every large village had its own ball court. Music and dance featured highly in the Arawak community. They made musical instruments such as drums from hollowed logs, and gourds filled with pebbles. They sang songs about their history and recorded events by drawing pictures on rocks or on cave walls.

Arawak society was highly organised and each village was in a district governed by a headman. Each district was in a province. Toward the end of the 15th century there were six provinces, two hundred districts, and over four hundred villages on the island of Hispaniola.

The village headman was under the sub- chief, who was answerable to the chief. 'The headman' planned the hunting and fishing trips and the cultivation. He was responsible for the keeping of stores of food so that if crops were scarce he could share out provisions among the villagers. The headman was also responsible for seeing that the law was obeyed . Crimes that were punishable by death were theft and adultery.

The chiefs were very powerful and were given great privileges. They wore gold ornaments whereas the common people wore wood, stone or bone.

THE CARIBS

It has been said that the Caribs were a warrior people usually arriving on the Caribbean Islands later than the Arawaks, whom they fought for control of territory. When the Caribs attacked the Arawaks they usually carried off the Arawak women.

Carib villages were built in positions that could be defended against attack, and were usually near a stream. Like the Arawaks they were subsistence farmers, and prided themselves on their fishing and hunting skills. As hunters and raiders they moved their villages frequently from one place to another. They loved water sports and their favourite was canoe-racing. Dancing and wrestling also formed apart of their leisure activities.

Carib chiefs were war chiefs elected by their people;

"to be elected, a man had to have shown that he was a fearless warrior, a good swimmer and diver, strong, and able to stand bodily injury without showing pain." Hall (ibid).

From a general point of view both the Arawaks and the Caribs were very similar in culture but each having strengths in different areas of their daily lives. For example the Caribs were excellent potters while the Arawaks were skilful in basket weaving, they were able to produce a basket suitable for carrying water, this was made by double -weaving wood and leaves.

As both sets of people were seamen their canoes was made with great skill without the aid of any metal tools.

"a wide silk cotton tree was first ringed and burnt off at the base.....the trunk was hollowed by chipping the upper side and slowly burning out the interior. The canoe was shaped by wetting the hollowed trunk.....it was then buried in damp sand to cure before being dried in the sun." Claypole (ibid).

COLUMBUS THE COLONISER

In 1492 Columbus sailed westwards across the Atlantic hoping to arrive in the Far East. When he reached the Bahamas he thought he had reached his destination, believing he was in the area of Japan, China and India. Hence his renaming of the islands he found the "West Indies".

"....To say that Columbus discovered America is a misuse of words. Columbus re-

vealed to Europeans the existence of the continents and islands which were inhabited already, and had been so for many centuries. Columbus did not discover a new world; he established contact between two worlds, both already old. More important, he did so at a time when the peoples of western Europe had recently developed ships and navigating instruments...." Sherlock (ibid)

In 1493, seventeen ships with 12,000 colonists set out from Spain to Hispaniola. The group took farming implements and seeds for planting.

"It was the largest colonizing expedition ever to have ever set out from Europe. (It) included priests, soldiers, officials...The expedition was instructed to convert the natives to the Catholic church, to develop trade between Hispaniola and Spain, and to explore Cuba..." Hall (ibid)

Once the Spanish had established themselves the Arawaks' way of life fundamentally changed. They were now the servants of the Spaniards; forced into the production of unfamiliar things for both the Spanish settlers on the island and Spanish merchants abroad. Their land and their leadership was taken from them. They were required to accept the strange customs and religious beliefs of the newcomers.

GOLD, RELIGION AND SUGAR: DEATH OF A NATION

C.L.R. James (9) in *'The Black Jacobins'* goes on to tell us how contact between the two worlds destroyed a nation:

" They (the Spanish) introduced Christianity, forced labour in mines, murder, rape, bloodhounds, strange diseases, and artificial famine (by the destruction of cultivation to starve the rebellious) These and other requirements of the higher civilization reduced the native population (of Hispaniola) from an estimated half-a- million, perhaps a million, to 60,000 in 15 years."

It is generally agreed that the arrival of the Europeans in the Caribbean decimated an entire nation but there are varying opinions as to the numbers of native people who were destroyed. Hans Koning (10) in *'Columbus: His Enterprise'* says,

".... an estimated one half of the entire population of Hispaniola was killed or killed themselves. The estimates run from one hundred and twenty five thousand to one half million." Koning (ibid).

Bartolome de las Casas, a friar who went to the Caribbean, gives an example of the horrors that took place,

" I have seen them burnt alive, torn to pieces, and put to all manner of elaborate torment. The tale of horrors is so long that I am not able to write it down...." (ibid).

After thirty years of Spanish settlement the population of Hispaniola had almost disappeared. The Spanish were desperate to find other forms of labour to work in the mines and on the plantations. Slave raids were made on The Bahamas, the Amerindians who were brought in also died.

The Spanish turned to African slaves. Such labour was not new to them; for more than a hundred years small numbers of Africans had been taken to Spain itself and later to the cane fields on the Canary islands. Hans Koning supports this by saying.

" The hardier black slaves from Africa were brought in to take their place. They would, at the end of the eighteenth century, stage the first and perhaps only successful slave revolt in Western history.... The death toll among blacks had been frightful too, but they had been brought in such numbers that enough of them survived to form a nation." (ibid)

Once transportation of slaves from Africa to the Caribbean had been established, people from the West African Gold Coast were preferred on account of their understanding of the art of land cultivation.

20

LEARNING OUTCOMES

The main aim of this section has been to show that, prior to the arrival of Europeans, African societies were civilized and highly advanced. They had their share of wars, disagreements and political differences. They took slaves, as did many countries, as spoils of war, but first and foremost African societies were ancient societies. They had political and economic structures, art, medicine, science and agriculture. The section reinforces these ideas and enables pupils and students to contrast the evidence with the ideas they may already have about African people.

a)   Through a careful reading of text, and through the participation in a number of exercises and activities pupils and students will be aware of the fact that there were sophisticated societies in Africa prior to the arrival of the Europeans.

b)   Pupils and students will know something of the art, culture, language and the structure of some of the ancient African societies.

c)   Pupils and students will be aware of the fact that modern man came out of Africa. They will be aware of the evidence to support this claim.

d)   Through a reading of relevant materials, pupils and students will understand certain concepts such as: tribe, civilization, ancient society and oral tradition. They will also be aware of the sheer size of the African continent and how this relates to its cultural, religious and political diversity.

e)   Pupils and students will be aware of the type of industry which existed in Kushite society and be able to give details of other African civilizations such as Ghana, Mali and North Africa.

f)   Through a close reading of maps and other visual materials, pupils and students will be able to locate African countries and say something about their physical geography.

NATIONAL CURRICULUM

A) Pupils and students will be able to draw out logical conclusions from primary and secondary source materials including maps, text, charts, tables, art and sculpture.

B) Pupils and students will be able to understand the relationship between historical events and contemporary situations. In relation to this section they will have an insight into the effect that successive European invasions had on the development of African countries.

C)   Through a reading of maps pupils and students will be able to 'grasp' the geographical relationship between Africa and Europe. They will understand that Africa is a continent with a number of independent countries within its borders.

D)   Teachers should encourage pupils and students to explore cross - curricular themes in Geography, English and Art.

E) Pupils and students, through the study of ancient African hieroglyphics, sculptures and cave paintings, will be able to assess the achievements and the extent of artistic, cultural and domestic development in early African societies.

F)   Teachers should build on pupils' knowledge of developing African and Caribbean countries, acquired through Key Stage Two in Geography.

Image:
Charles Cordier.
'Negre Du Darfour'

REFERENCES

(1) **Basil Davidson** *'African Kingdoms'*. Pub by Time Inc. 1967.

(2) *'Encyclopedia Britannica.'*

(3) **M.Shinnie** *'Ancient African Kingdoms'* (out of print). Pub by Edwards & Arnold 1965.

(4) **A. Sundel** *'A History Of The Aztecs And The Mayas And Their Conquests.'* Published by Macmillan in 1967.

(5) **Sherlock, Parry & Maingot** *'A Short History Of The West Indies'* Published By Macmillan 1987.

(6) **D.Hall** *'The Caribbean Experience'*. Published by Heinemann 1982.

(7) **Claypole & Robottom** *'Caribbean Story - Book One: Foundation'*. Pub By Longmans 1986.

(8) **P. Hulme & N.L. Whitehead** *'Wild Majesty.' Clarendon* Press 1992.

(9) **C.L.R. James** *'The Black Jacobins - Toussaint L'Ouverture And The San Domingo Revolution'*. Alison & Bushby 1991.

(10) **Hans Koning** *'Columbus - His Enterprise'. 'Latin* American Bureau 1976.

Background image, Maya Angelou - 1997

BLACK PEOPLE IN BRITAIN

The main aim of this section is to look at the issue of the historical presence of Black people in Britain, and specifically in Liverpool. Through this section it will become clear that slaves were sold in Britain and that there is evidence to show this, particularly through the advertisements from local Liverpool newspapers in the 18th century. This is an important point, for it serves to challenge the notion that slaves were never sold in mainland Britain.

It is true to say that slaves were never sold in Liverpool in the same way that they were sold in Africa and in the Caribbean; there were, for example, no sales through private treaty or barter and there were no sales through "the scramble" (1); however, there were regular sales of slaves through public auction. Many coffee house advertisements and notices in the 'Liverpool Williamson's Advertiser' (2) provide clear evidence of this.

Prior to the 18th century there had already been a Black presence in Britain: the Spanish and Portuguese were known to have brought Africans to Britain from the 14th century onwards, and in 1555 John Lok brought a small group of Black slaves to England:

> "Suddenly the African was no longer a curiosity from the pages of traveller's tales but a living reality on the streets of London. After Lok's voyage, the traffic in black slaves expanded rapidly, and by the end of the century black servants were a common sight throughout the country." (3)

There have been Africans in Europe from the time of classical antiquity and one of the earliest records of Africans in Britain dates from the period of the Roman occupation. During the 3rd century AD there was a unit of African troops, the "numerus Maurorum", (loosely translated means "many Blacks"), stationed near Carlisle. This troop probably numbered several hundred. As Edwards notes (4):

> "... there is no reason to think that on their discharge from the army that they returned to their homes."

This being the case it is possible to speculate about the ancestry of the people of Scotland. On this point MacRitchie states, when discussing ancient Scottish legends:

> "... the popular tales of the West Highlands are full of dark skinned people, whose deeds are often recited by people half-conscious of the fact that they, too, are anything but white." (5)

Mac Ritchie provides further evidence of a Black presence in Scotland prior to the Roman occupation. Writing in 1884 he provides evidence from the work of ancient scholars and from the work of his contemporaries, he states:

> "Professor Huxley, speaking on this subject, says 'that probably in the time of Caesar, and certainly in that of Tacitus, there existed in these islands two distinct types of population: the one of tall stature, with fair skin, yellow hair and blue eyes; the other of short stature, with dark skin [as dark as an Ethiopian's says Pliny; as dark as a "Moor's" , says Claudian] dark hair, dark eyes'.... Thus, the "British" , whom the Romans encountered, were made up of ingredients as greatly different from each other as are the component parts of the present day population of the United States. They were, at least, fair whites, dark whites, and blacks."

Africans also found their way into Medieval Britain. As recorded in an ancient Irish chronicle a "...great host" of Black slaves from North Africa were brought to Ireland in 862 AD by Vikings who had settled there. The Vikings, having raided Spain and North Africa, had taken their captives to Ireland (Edwards ibid). Evidence of a Black presence in Ireland, and in Scotland, at this time is further supported through the work of MacRitchie (ibid). He argues:

> *".... not only were there Black people in Britain during the dark ages (dark in a double sense), but also they constituted, or at least formed a recognised part of, the class of wandering minstrels and mountebanks."*

The history of Black people in Britain certainly goes back a long way. It is one which should be undertood in terms of 'waves'. That is to say that there have been different Black communities here at specific points in time, from the movement of modern man out of Africa (approximately 50,000 years ago) to the recent arrival in Britain of people from East Africa in the 1990s. The main point of differentiation between these 'waves' relates to the impetus behind the movement.

In 1596 there was a general concern that there were too many Black people in the country and that they were taking food from the mouths of true British subjects. This was summed up in the famous proclamation made by Queen Elizabeth I when she ordered the deportation of ".. *A great number of Negroes and Blackamores which are carried into the realm*" .(6) Similarly on April 5th 1723, the *'London Daily Journal'* reported on the influx of Black people in the country and the fear of being "swamped" by them:

> *"'tis said there is a great number of Blacks come daily into the city, so that 'tis thought in a short time, if they not be suppress'd, the city will swarm with them."* *Dabydene (ibid).*

The fear of being swamped has stayed with the white community from the 1500s until the present day. It was the fear of the anti-Black rioters in Liverpool in 1919 and 1948; it was used by right wing extremists in the 1950s and 60s; by Margaret Thatcher in the late 1970s and it has been used by Conservative Members of Parliament in the 1980s and the 1990s.

The development of British colonies in the 'New World' in the 17th century was to be the basis for the expanding Black population in Britain

of that time. From 1655, when the British secured Jamaica as a colony and it became a major clearing house for slaves, the Black population in Britain began to grow. It was common for overseers to send their ("mulatto") children back to England to be educated. As Rogers (7) puts it:

> *" ..so many mulatto offspring went to England to study... the son is sent to Westminster or Eton while the daughter is sent to Chelsea or some famed seminary."*

Initially it was London and Bristol, but particularly London, which had a sizable Black community. Towards the end of the 18th century Liverpool, however, had emerged as the British leader in the trade in slaves. Generally speaking as Liverpool's involvement in slavery increased throughout the 1700s, so its Black population continued to grow. By 1760 the Black population in Britain was variously estimated at between 20,000 and 40,000.

In the 18th and 19th centuries Black people were a common feature of British society; this is noted in the work of Hogarth and in that of other 18th century painters. Several of the better known Black personalities of thes period have been immortalised in the history books. Personalities such as the writers Olaudah Equiano and Ignatius Sancho, characters like the street entertainer Billy Waters and the beggar Joseph Johnson. Well known Black boxers of the period include Bill Richmond and Tom Molineaux. Of the Black women we know of there was Saartjie Bartman, the so-called *"Hottentot Venus"*, poetess Phillis Wheatley and nurse Mary Seacole. Black people in England survived on their wits and, in some instances, became a part of the new rural poor.

Many Liverpool planters having made their fortunes in the Caribbean, left their plantations to be managed by overseers and became absent landlords. They then returned to England *"in a style which outshone the aristocracy" (Walvin Ibid).* They were often accompanied by Black slaves and servants. Also, as Fryer (ibid) points out, captains, surgeons, mates and other higher ranking officers short on funds often converted their *"privilege negro"* into a spot of ready cash by selling them. Hence advertisements in the *'Liverpool Williamson's Advertiser'* and the *'Liverpool Chronicle'* giving details of the sale of such slaves.

During the 18th and 19th centuries there was some confusion in English law about slavery. Whether it was, or was not, permissible in this country. On the one hand the Habeas Corpus Act of 1679 appeared to guarantee basic human rights to all individuals, irrespective of racial origin. On the other hand Black people were viewed as chattel, property which could be moved from one location to another (as defined by the Navigation Acts).

In 1706 Lord Justice Hold declared

> *".. by common law no man can have property in another... there is no such a thing as a slave by the laws of England." Edwards & Walvin (ibid)*

Opinions in 1729 and 1745 declared the reverse. In 1745 Lord Hardwicke held that,

> *".. a slave, even though baptised, remains the property of his master, and could return from England to slavery in the colonies at his will." (ibid)*

Such battles raged over the status of Black people in Britain in the 18th century. They were largely a question of interpretation, with individuals forwarding arguments which would best serve their particular interests. The position of the slave traders in this argument was clear. The view of the status of a Black person in the 18th century is very much related to ideology and propaganda. We will return to this issue when looking at *'Slavery and Ideology - A Legacy Of The Past'*.

SLAVE SALES IN BRITAIN

Britain had no direct economic need for slaves, or servants; though they were essential to the economic expansion of European settlements in the Americas, so why were they in Britain in the 18th century? Initially curiosity might explain the importation of Black people into Britain. But thereafter they became fashion accessories. This was confirmed by the widespread use of Black domestics, stable hands, servants, butlers and the like. Black people performed these duties for the landed aristocracy and the new industrial and colonial classes despite the fact that there was never a shortage of indigenous white labour available

to perform them equally as well. It must also be remembered that Black people were not paid for their labour - the initial asking price, once paid, enabled the owner to use of a slave for any purpose.

The symbolic status of Black people in the 18th century can be accurately gauged from the family paintings and portraits of the time. These paintings were tokens of family affluence and colonial business interests. And though the status of the Black person in the family household was only equal to that of the lap dog, the pet lamb or the favourite horse, and sometimes less, they were clearly visible. By the mid 18th century the practice of using Blacks as domestics became widespread. This encouraged slave traders to sell small numbers of Black slaves in, and around, British ports.

Slaves were sold through the columns of local newspapers alongside other commodities and in much the same way as their brothers and sisters in Africa and the Caribbean, though clearly not on the same scale. One Liverpool street witnessed so many sales of Black children and youths that it was nicknamed "Negro Roe" or "Negro Street". African slaves were sold by auction in shops, warehouses, coffee houses and on the steps of Custom House on the east side of the Old Liverpool Dock (now Canning Place). As Dicky Sam puts it,

> *".. in 1766 the chief topic of interest on the Liverpool Exchange Flags were the price of slaves, sugars and rum: the former articles of merchandise occasionally being sold on the Custom House steps."*

LEARNING OUTCOMES

a) Pupils and students will be aware that there has been a Black presence in the British Isles for many centuries, the first recorded presence being before the Roman occupation.

b) Pupils and students, through a close reading of primary and secondary source materials, will know the various roles that Black people played in British society in the 17th,18th and 19th centuries.

c) Through discussion and further research, pupils and students will be able to articulate the status of Black people in British society in the 18th century. They will be able to engage into a debate as to whether they were free, or chattel.

d) Through an examination of the evidence presented in Part Two and further research, pupils and students will be familiar with the details of slave sales in Liverpool and other parts of the country. This is important as it challenges notions that slaves were never sold in Britain. It will be important for teachers and educators to detail the difference between slave sales in Britain, and sales in Africa and the Caribbean.

e) Pupils and students will begin to think from the point of view of Black people in 18th century Britain. They should, through exercises and activities, be able to gain an insight, and an empathy, into the experience of Black people in Britain during this period.

NATIONAL CURRICULUM.

(A) Pupils and students will begin to draw their own conclusions based on evidence, through a reading of relevant primary and secondary source materials.

(B) Pupils and students will critically evaluate the evidence. Understanding, for example, that there is more than one interpretation of an historical fact and that the best conclusions are to be drawn from the best evidence. If evidence is conflicting, then pupils and students should be able to present logical arguments in support of their opinion.

(C) As a cross curricular theme pupils and students should explore the geographical relationship between Africa, the Caribbean and Europe and carry out further research.

REFERENCES

(1)　**Dicky Sam** *'Liverpool And Slavery'* Centinary Edition published by Scouse Press 1984. First Published in 1884.

(2)　Late 18th Century Newspapers: *'The Williamson's Advertiser'* - August 20th 1756; 'The Liverpool Chronicle' - 1750s.

(3)　**David Dabydene** - *'Hogarth's Blacks - Images of Blacks in Eighteenth Century English Art'*. Dangaroo Press 1985

(4)　**P. Edwards & J. Walvin** - *'Black Personalities In The Era Of The Slave Trade'* - Macmillan Press 1983.

(5)　**D. MacRitchie** -*'Ancient And Modern Britons'*. Vol 1 Keegan Paul 1884.

(6)　**P. Fryer** - *'Staying Power- A History of Black* People In Britain' Pluto Press 1984.

(7)　**J.A. Rogers** -*'Sex And Race'* Vol 2 Helga.A.Rogers 1942.

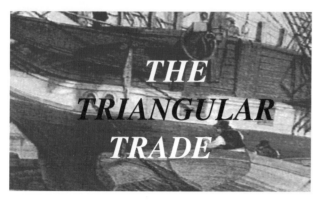

INTRODUCTION

The so-called 'Triangular Trade' of slavery refers to the voyages made by European ships to the West Coast of Africa, the Americas and back to Europe. The term 'triangular' refers to the three distinct parts of the journey. The main focus for this section will be on Britain: what goods were manufactured and transported to Africa; where they were manufactured and how they were bartered on the ships arrival in Africa. Details of slave sales in Africa, what goods were produced and exchanged in the Caribbean and how profit was accrued through this process will also be explored.

The immediate background to the triangular trade relates to the demand of the British people for sugar and the need to acquire labour in order for its production in the British colonies in the Caribbean. The British had long since made contact with African people through the voyages of Thomas Windham who sailed from Portsmouth to Guinea and Benin (modern Nigeria) in 1553. His voyage was soon to be followed by John Lok in 1554 and Sir John Hawkins in 1555.

In addition to the new British taste for sugar, before there could be a profitable triangular trade there needed to be a firm base for the production of goods to be traded on the West African coast. By the early 1700s the major British towns were in a position to produce sufficient goods, textiles, metals, food stuffs etc., for export to Africa. The fact that Liverpool was late to enter into this trade reflects the fact, to some extent, that it was not in a position to provide surplus goods for trade until the early 1700s with the first voyage of the 'Blessing' in 1701. Liverpool's late arrival was also due to the fact that companies such as 'The Royal African Assiento Company' had a monopoly on the trade, one which it was not prepared to relinquish until 1698. Early in the 18th century:

"...a successful rivalship with Bristol, in exporting provisions, and coarse checks and silk handkerchiefs of Manchester make, to the West Indies and the continent of America, eventually enabled the merchants of Liverpool to participate in the more lucrative slave traffic. While Liverpool obtained from this competition a sudden accession to her commerce, which stimulated the industrious and enriched the enterprising, multiplied the ships in her docks, and filled her warehouses with sugar, rum and other West Indian produce, the trade of Bristol to the West Indies declined." Gomer Williams (1).

Although we are most concerned with the Triangular slave trade in this section, it should also be mentioned that before the triangular trade there was a bilateral trade between some European countries and Africa. The Americas were not always a part of the trading equation. Liverpool merchants, for example, bought ivory, palm oil and bronze (from Benin) from African traders in exchange for British manufactured goods. Liverpool's Oil Street stands as a reminder of the bilateral trade in palm oil.

THE TRIANGULAR TRADE

The triangular trade worked in such a way that there was scope for profit at each of its stages. Ships would leave the main slave trading towns of London, Bristol and Liverpool loaded with goods to be traded: textiles made in Lancashire; cutlery made in Birmingham; bronze rings made in Warrington and St Helens. Cargos would also include tobacco, spirits and beers brewed by Whitbread and Truemans. When ships arrived on the coast of Africa the captain and members of his crew would row inland using small 'long-boats'. It would be the responsibility of the ship's captain to barter with various traders in order to get the best deal. This would mean getting as many Africans as possible for the smallest, or least valuable exchange.(see Biard's painting *'The Slave Trade'*).

There were several ways that were commonly used in order to catch slaves, most of which relied on the captains' ability to bribe or trick tribal leaders or to take advantage of tribal rivalry by introducing guns and other weaponry into (one side) of a local conflict. Sam (2) gives some detail as to how slaves were caught in Calabar. This often involved bribing local chiefs to make war on their neighbours. The usual scenario would be for one tribe to ambush another during the night:

> " *Accra's men rushed into the villages with lighted torches, and set fire to anything that would burn, making at the same time the most hideous yells to frighten and terrify the peaceful Negroes within their huts and cabins. It was not long before the two villages were in flames, out rushed the frightened negroes for safety, when they were immediately pounced on by Accra's men, and bound hand and foot with ropes and chains, and then thrown into the canoes. In this way they would kidnap as many as fifty and a hundred men at a time. Down the river as fast as they can go , with their living cargo, to the good ship 'Thomas' of Liverpool.*"

Another method of obtaining slaves was by inviting African traders to come on board the ship and dine with the captain:

> " *when they were well supplied with drink, the ship would be got under-way, all sails set, and rapidly leave the shore. The traders on awaking would find themselves out at sea; they would be stripped, branded, and put down the hold to share the fate of other slaves.*" *Sam (ibid).*

Such acts were justified by slave traders for, after all most slaves were criminals, or undesirables who, had they not been 'rescued' by slave traders, would have been put to death. Of the crimes of the guilty Mathieson (3) recognises the fraility of such 'logic':

> "*With a hellish ingenuity the very crimes of the country seemed to have been made on purpose to serve the interests of slave-sellers and slave buyers. Theft, adultry,witchcraft and the removal of fetiches were falsely imputed for the sake of selling the accused into slavery, and some of the chief men were said to employ the best looking women they could find, well dressed, in order to entice the unwary into criminal*

> *situations, which ensured their conviction, or offered a pretext for selling them to Europeans.*"

Compounds were erected on the beach near the slave trading centres; into these Africans were herded, merchants having previously shaved their heads so as to disguise their actual age. Their bodies were rubbed with palm oil to give an appearance of sleekness and vitality. In the compounds they were stripped naked and examined. The ship's doctor had an important role to play. It was he who had the final say in what slaves were bought. His job was to ensure that the majority of the slaves he selected would be able to survive the long voyage from the coast of Africa to America and the Caribbean. He also had to be careful not to choose slaves who would cause trouble either on board ship or in the plantations by refusing to work. The Africans bought by the European slave traders were mostly very young able-bodied men and women between the age of 15 and 25. 'Cargoes' often included a proportion of children, *"but people over the age of 30 were almost always rejected." (4)*

Those slaves passed as fit and healthy were then branded, *"on the breast, buttock or back, according to the fancy of the brander"* with the purchasing company's mark. The reason for the branding was to prevent the slave traders exchanging the approved slaves for unfit ones during the marshalling in the compounds prior to shipment. The branding also provided information to the buyers in the Caribbean and America as to the likely quality of the slaves, as over time certain brands became associated with quality, both good and poor.

> " *The Liverpool brand, DD, burnt with red hot irons into the living flesh of African men, women and children, was famous among West Indian planters as a guarantee of prime quality.*" (5)

The slaves were then forced onto the waiting slavers shackled in pairs in leg irons. The slave ship would probably have had to sail to several different locations before it had bought enough slaves to fill up its hull. This part of the voyage could take anything from six to eight months. Once the captain was satisfied with his cargo, the ship would begin the second leg of the voyage, the notorious 'Middle Passage'. This part of the journey could prove to be most problematic for captains in terms of loss of slaves through disease, rebellion of slaves (and slaves jumping overboard) and attacks from privateers and pirates.

In Barbados, the Leeward Islands, Jamaica and Surinam these young Africans were sold as slaves. Deals were done through auction and slaves were exchanged for cash, or they were exchanged for agreed amounts of sugar, rum, spices, molasses and tobacco. Other slaves were sold through a 'lottery system' called the 'scramble'. This method of sale would involve a captain leaving his 'cargo' in the hold of the ship, or under cover of canvas on the deck of the ship. All buyers would then purchase a ticket , this would entitle them, on orders, to storm the ship and grab the best of the available cargo.

All goods bought in the Caribbean would be brought back to England or to whichever European country the ship had made her sailing from. With a proportion of the profit more manufactured goods were bought, and the cycle began afresh:

"It was an ingenious system, for the ships never needed to travel empty. And it was an enormously profitable system for the planters whose slaves produced the sugar, the merchant capitalists who sold them the slaves, the industrial capitalists who supplied the manufactured goods with which the slaves were bought, and the bankers and commission agents who lent money to all of them." Fryer (ibid).

Manchester and the textile industries prospered, with many companies producing cotton goods, guns and cutlery specifically for export to Africa. It has been estimated that by the mid 1700s almost half of the cotton manufactured in Lancashire was produced specifically to be traded for slaves in Africa. There can be no doubt that slavery provided a "shot in the arm" for British manufacturing and that it spurred on the Industrial Revolution whilst attracting the rural poor out of the country side and into the mills and foundries. And whilst there is much controversy in relation to the extent to which slavery and the threefold profits

of the triangular trade financed Britain's Industrial Revolution, that it had a hand in it cannot be denied. As Fryer (Ibid) notes, from the work of Eric Williams, slavery and the making of industrialised Britain went hand in hand:

" Rising British capitalism had a magic money machine, an endless chain with three links: sugar cultivation; manufacturing industry; and the slave trade. And the slave trade was the 'essential link'. The whole system 'was frankly regarded as resting on slavery'."

Williams further states in *'From Columbus To Castro'* (6) :

"The slave trade kept the wheels of metropolitan industry turning; it stimulated navigation and ship building and employed seamen; it raised fishing villages into flourishing cities; it gave sustenance to new industries based on the processing of colonial raw materials; it yielded large profits which were ploughed back into metropolitan industry; and, finally, it gave rise to an unprecedented commerce in the West Indies and made the Caribbean territories among the most valuable colonies the world has ever known."

LEARNING OUTCOMES

a) Through careful reading of the text, through participation in exercises and activities and through the study of primary and secondary source information, pupils and students will be able to understand what the Triangular Trade was and how it worked.

b) Pupils and students will be aware of the detail of each side of the Triangular Trade, that is: the goods which were traded on the coast of Africa; how trade took place in Africa; what the Middle Passage was; how slaves were sold in the Caribbean and Americas; the goods which were brought back to England and how this process was self generating.

c) Pupils and students will be aware of the debate vis-a-vis the relationship between the slave trade and industrialisation in Britain.

d) Pupils and students, through a series of exercise and activities, will be able to challenge their own presuppositions about the triangular trade.

e) Pupils and students will be in a position to assess the impact that slavery had on Africa and understand that current underdevelopment in African counties, and in the Caribbean, is inextricably linked to the slave trade - this is evident in Jamaica which has never been fully developed due to its reliance on a single crop economy, sugar. This reliance is historical and relates to the demand for sugar in Britain and in Europe in the 1700s.

f) Through further research pupils should gain information on life in the Caribbean prior to the arrival of Africans. They should know that there was an indigenous population in the Caribbean prior to the arrival of the Spanish, Portuguese, British etc., and something about what happened to the population. This information will help to reinforce the knowledge acquired by pupils and students from Section Three.

NATIONAL CURRICULUM

A) Pupils and students will be able to understand the relationship between historical events and contemporary situations.

B) Pupils and students will, through research and exploration of their own environments, be able to identify 'clues' which give information about the past. Pupils and students should be encouraged to examine and research: street names; buildings; monuments and district names.

C) Pupils should be able to understand the motivation of those involved in the slave trade in order to have a clearer idea of why they behaved as they did. This is important when looking at: why Africans sold members of opposing tribes, and their own tribes, to Europeans, and why Europeans travelled to Africa in the first place.

D) Through a full reading of text and primary and secondary source materials pupils and students will be able to draw out important information and assess its validity.

E) Pupils and students will be able to develop a sense of empathy - they will be able to imagine what the experience of slavery might have been like and how slavery disrupted the family, and tribal lives of so many Africans.

F) Pupils and students should be able to grasp, geographically, the relationships between the countries under investigation: Britain, Europe, Africa, America and the Caribbean.

REFERENCES

(1)   **G.Williams** *The Liverpool Privateers With An Account Of The Liverpool Slave Trade'* Heinemann 1891.

(2)   **Dicky Sam** *'Liverpool and Slavery'.* Centenary Edition Scouse Press 1984 - First Pulished 1884.

(3)   **William Mathieson** *'Great Britain And The Slave Trade 1839-1865'* Longman, Green & Co 1929.

(4)   **Peter Fryer** *'Black People In The British Empire - An Introduction'.* Pluto Press 1984.

(5)   **Peter Fryer** *'Staying Power - A History Of Black People In Britain'.* Pluto Press 1983.

(6)   **Eric Williams** - *'From Columbus To Castro - A History of The Caribbean 1492-1969.' Published in 1970 by Andre Deutsch.*

THE MIDDLE PASSAGE

*"Freighted with curses was the
dark that bore the spoilers of the
West To Guinea's shore; Heavy
with groans of anguish blew the
gails that swelled that fatal
barks sails; Old Ocean shrunk,
as o'er his surface flew the
human cargo and the demon crew." (1)*

INTRODUCTION

There are several aims to this section: the most important of which is to try and convey to pupils and students the sheer horror and misery of the Middle Passage. The conditions aboard ship and the treatment of slaves will be looked at through a careful reading of several accounts of the Middle Passage.

Also in this section pupils and students should gain an insight into how slaves were viewed, that is as a commodity to be traded in the Americas; and exactly how the Middle Passage formed an integral part of the Triangular Trade.

Unlike preceding sections, this section is presented in the form of a number of short summaries of the work of various writers. Each piece serves to make a number of points about the Middle Passage. All are reproduced in full in Part Two. Teachers and educationalists should give pupils and students the opportunity of reading as many accounts of the Middle Passage as possible and then use the points made in this section as the basis for further discussion.

THE MIDDLE PASSAGE

Several writers acknowledge the difficulty in capturing the true horror of the slave trade and the dreadful voyage of despair taken by so many millions of Africans. They were, in some instances, marched to the coast of a great ocean which they had never seen, separated from their loved ones by strange white men whose motivation they could not begin to imagine and then, having suffered the indignity of being sold, and the pain of being branded, packed into the dark holds of murderous ships. There began the Middle Passage which is typically characterised as a passage of indignity, dehumanisation, misery, disease and death

The extracts presented are written at different times. Most were written over 50 years ago. The Dicky Sam extract was written in 1884 (2), the William Law Mathieson in 1929 (3) and the C.L.R. James extract was written in 1934 (4). All of these extracts were written by scholars who had direct access to primary source materials. Many use quotes from captains, abolitionists and others who were contemporaries of the slave trade.

The only extract which comes from an individual who actually experienced slavery, and therefor the Middle Passage, is that taken from Olaudah Equiano's book, *'Interesting Narrative'* (5). Extracts from this book appear in several chapters.

DICKY SAM
'Liverpool and Slavery'

Whilst this extract focuses on the experience of slaves during the Middle Passage: what they eat, how they were treated and the diseases which some succumbed to, it also gives us a little insight into how the Middle Passage fits into the wider Triangular Trade. We are told about: the cargo that was initially on board and traded for slaves in Africa; how much the slaves were sold for on arrival in Kingston Jamaica; what goods were taken back to Liverpool; who profited, and by how much; the role of business men and bankers and the timescale of the 'operation' from start to finish.

Sam's extract is interesting because it is written from the point of view of someone who would have known people whose fathers had been directly involved in the slave trade; it was for this reason he wrote under a pseudonym. There is also a compassion in Sam's writing which informs us of the horror of the slave trade; so that whilst he describes the slave trade and how it operated in terms of profit and loss, he also describes the cost in human misery and suffering. He summarises the voyage of the 'Thomas' and gives a precis of the Triangular Trade from a retrospective and tragic point of view:

> *"What an eventful voyage it has been - first with her cargo of trumpery, trinkets, pistols, muskets, gun-powder, cutlasses, and such like; these bartered for living beings, villages set on fire, wars made between non-offending people, menstealers prowling about the country, a thousand subterfuges resorted to, in order to kidnap the poor negroes. Women torn from their suckling infants, sons and daughters from fathers and mothers, and humanity outraged in the name of religion."*

C.L.R. JAMES
'The Black Jacobins'

The chapter reproduced from 'The Black Jacobins' is called 'The Property'. It serves to challenge erroneous notions about the role that Africans played in the slave trade while at the same time giving an insight into the way that African societies functioned prior to the arrival of Europeans.

The Slave Trade, it is said, was carried out with,

> *"...the active participation of African chiefs ... cruelty and inhumanity of man to man knows no colour distinctions."*
> (6).

As James explains:

> *"the tribal wars from which European pirates claimed to deliver the people were mere sham-fights; it was a great fight when half a dozen men were killed."*

Europeans took advantage of tribal rivalry through the provision of muskets, cutlasses and gunpowder and eventually detribalised great regions of Africa. African chiefs had to supply slaves or be sold themselves. The horrors that took place in Africa: human sacrifice, the selling of children and family were, *"the product of an intolerable pressure on the African peoples"*.

There was slavery in Africa prior to the European arrival, indeed slavery is an historic institution (see *'Slavery Through The Ages'*). However, African chiefs could never have imagined the kind of slavery into which they were forced to sell their brothers and sisters.

'The Black Jacobins' has one central theme running through it, and that is the theme of African self-liberation from slavery; how they made the system unworkable and how a great slave revolution led by Toussaint L'Ouverture led to the establishment of *...the Negro state of Haiti."*

James describes the horrors of the Middle Passage and the manner in which slave ship captains put down revolutions and dissuaded slaves from contemplating escape. James also shows that, for slaves, death was a powerful alternative to their unknown and mysterious destination. It also offered the possibility of rebirth, and a new life in more familiar surroundings - namely, Africa.

WILLIAM MATHIESON
'Great Britain and The Slave Trade'

This short extract gives details about the intolerable conditions under which the slaves endured the Middle Passsage:

> *"...packed often so closely that they sat between each others legs; they were chained by the ankle in pairs, their fetters being, not locked, but riveted; and the boarding above them was in so many cases so low that they could not even sit upright."*

It is possible to get an impression of just how cramped these conditions would have been through looking at the reproduction of the 'Brookes', and its dimentions, presented in the supplementary materials for this section.

The 'Brookes' was legally allowed to carry 450 slaves, but regularly carried many more than this. So small was the space allowed for each slave that they had less room than they would have had, had they been in coffins.

Mathieson describes the effect that such cramped conditions, coupled with a lack of food and water, had on the slaves and the nature of the diseases which they invariably succumbed to.

OLAUDAH EQUIANO
'Interesting Narrative'
or 'Equiano's Travels'

The extract from Olaudah Equiano's book describes slavery from the point of view of someone who actually experienced it. When Equiano was 10 or 11 he was captured in Africa, taken to the Benin coast and then transported to Barbados. Equiano was then transported a second time to Virginia before ending up as a servant to a ship's captain. Equiano was re-sold into slavery in 1763 having been baptised, and having lived in London for a short time. Eventually Equiano was able to buy his freedom in 1766 after which he became a merchant seaman for eleven years. Equiano was an avid antislavery campaigner. He wrote the story of his life in 1789 and travelled extensively speaking out against the slave trade. Equiano married Susan Cullen, a woman from Ely in Cambridgeshire, in 1792. Having died in 1801, Equiano did not live to see the abolition of the trade which parted him forever from his homeland. The extract from Equiano's book further details the horror of the Middle Passage. The extract also enables us to share Equiano's sheer mystification about the situation he finds himself in. Everything is strange to him: the ocean; the people and the way in which they are dressed, their skin colour and hair; the ship itself and all of the new and fearful sights, smells and sensations which assault his senses once he boards ship. After Equiano is carried on board ship he describes his thoughts and fears:

"..I was now persuaded that I had gotten into the world of bad spirits, and that they were going to kill me. Their complexion too differing so much from ours, their long hair, and the language they spoke .... when I looked around the ship too and saw a large furnace or copper boiling, and a multitude of black people of every description chained together, every one of their countenance expressing objection of sorrow, I no longer doubted my fate; and quite overpowered with horror and anguish, I fell motionless on the deck and fainted."

The Middle Passage was truly a passage of terror and death. It was also an essential part of the Triangular Trade. As stated in the introduction, writers have found it difficult to convey the sheer horror of the Middle Passage. Gomer Williains, writing in 1897 acknowledges this and states:

" The mind cannot realise, language cannot paint the suffering of one day, nay one hour, passed under such circumstance, by the tightly-wedged human cargo in the hold of the best managed ship. Dreadful must have been the agony under the most favourable conditions, like John Newton, an able surgeon, fine weather, and a short passage, but what a circumscribed hell were they tormented in when after several months spent on the coast to complete the cargo, they experienced, during a long passage to the West Indies, lasting from six to eight weeks, rough weather, inhuman treatment, and scanty rations of bad quality! " Williams (Ibid).

Olaudah Equiano came to England as a slave in 1757, he was a tireless campaigner against the slave trade.

LEARNING OUTCOMES

Pupils will be aware of the sheer horror of the Middle Passage and gain a detailed knowledge (and insight) into the experience of the individuals who made the journey from Africa to the Americas. Such an awareness will be gained through a close reading of the texts presented in Part Two.

a) Pupils and students will understand how the Middle Passage formed part of the Triangle Trade.

b) Pupils and students will be able to locate Europe, the Americas and Africa on a map and, in spatial terms, demonstrate their understanding of the geographical relationships between these continents.

c) Pupils and students will be aware of how Africans rebelled on board ship and how such rebellions were put down.

d) From Equiano's work in particular, pupils and students will be able to gain an insight into what the middle Passage was really like.

NATIONAL CURRICULUM

(A) Through primary and secondary source materials pupils and students will be able to draw their own conclusions about the nature of the Middle Passage. They will also be in a position to evaluate information about it in a logical manner.

(B) Pupils and students will be able to critically evaluate the evidence, understanding the differing perspectives which writers bring to bear on their accounts of the Middle Passage. They will be aware that differing perspectives can mean differing interpretations of the same event.

(C) As part of a cross curricular theme pupils and students should look at the geographical relationship between Africa, the Caribbean and Britain. Through English they can improve their ability to write discursive essays and imaginative prose.

(D) Through a close reading of text and through participation in exercises and activities, pupils and students will be able to improve their comprehension skills.

REFERENCES

(1) **Gomer Williams** *'The Liverpool Privateers - With An account Of The Liverpool Slave Trade.'* Published by Heinemann 1897.

(2) **Dicky Sam** *'Liverpool And Slavery.'* Centenary Edition Scouse Press 1984. First Published in 1884.

(3) **William Law Mathieson** *'Great Britain and The Slave Trade 1839 1865.'* Longmans & Green 1929.

(4) **C.L.R. James** *'The Black Jacobins - Toussaint L'Ouverature And The San Domingo Revolution.'* Virgin Publishing, Copyright 1938.

(5) **Olaudah Equiano** *'Interesting Narrative.'* Printed in: Edwards & Walvin - *'Black Personalities In The Era Of The Slave Trade.'* Macmillan 1983.

(6) **Fritz Spiegel** in foreword to Dicky Sam's *'Liverpool And Slavery .'* I Centenary Edition 1984.

Trumpeters. Taken from a painted roll of a Westminster tournament held in 1511 to celebrate the birth of a son to Catherine of Aragon. The Black trumpeter is probably John Blanke

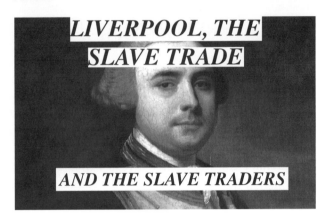

LIVERPOOL, THE SLAVE TRADE

AND THE SLAVE TRADERS

INTRODUCTION

There can be little doubt of the extent to which Liverpool profited from the slave trade; so much so that it has been described as *"the capital of the slave trade"*(1) and slavery has been described as *"the Eldorado of the Period"* (2) of the city's history from the mid 18th century to the early 19th. From local history books, the reluctance of educators to talk about slavery and the way in which public institutions, particularly museums, have been economical with the truth, people can be forgiven for underestimating the direct involvement that prominent individuals had in the trade in slaves. Slavery also created an important economic base upon which the City was able to build.

In this section we explore the extent to which Liverpool was involved in the slave trade. We also examine the profit accrued for the city and for prominant individuals.

LIVERPOOL AND THE SLAVE TRADE

At the height of the slave trade most of Liverpool's industries were either directly or indirectly involved in supplying goods to slave merchants to be traded in Africa. This included small speculators as well as Members of Parliament, Lord Mayors, bankers and the clergy:

" Almost every man in Liverpool is a merchant, and he who cannot send a bail, will send a bandbox ... The attractive African meteor has ...so dazzled their ideas,that almost every order of people is interested in a Guinea cargo ... It is well known that many of the small vessels that import about a hundred slaves, are fitted out by attornies, drapers, ropers, grocers, tallow-chandlers, barbers, taylors, etc.... Some have one-eighth, some a fifteenth and some a thirty-second." Fryer (ibid).

One of Liverpool's most famous historians, Ramsey Muir, has argued that without slavery Liverpool would have remained much as it had been towards the end of 17th century, a small insignificant seaport consisting of a few streets some distance from the creek, or pool, which served as the harbour. It was the slave trade that created new markets to exploit and *"flooded the town with wealth... (it) invigorated every industry"*, changing Liverpool forever from a struggling port to one of the richest trading centres in Europe.

There are differences in opinion when it comes to identifying a date from which Liverpool became directly involved in the slave trade. Some sources have suggested that the slave trade did not play any significant role in the economic development in the city before 1760 (3). Although Liverpool entered the slave trade relatively late, with London being involved through John Hawkins as early as 1555, it soon made up the lag and by the 1740s became the leading slave trading centre in Britain.

The first recorded voyage of a slaving ship took place in September 1700, when the 'Liverpool Merchant' sailed to Barbados. This ship was captained by William Webster and delivered 220 slaves from Africa to Barbados. They were sold for £4,239. The next month the 'Blessing' sailed under Captain Thomas Brownhill. In 1703 the 'Rebecca' also made a slaving voyage. It is by no means certain that these were Liverpool's first slaving ventures. It was in the interest of ships' Captains to falsify cargo records in order avoid paying the ten percent export duty which was chargeable at the time.

As a direct result of Liverpool's increasing involvement in the slave trade its population grew from 5,000 at the beginning of the 18th century to 78, 000 at its end. Neither Bristol, nor London had witnessd such a population increase during this period.

PROFITS AND THE SLAVE TRADERS

By the mid 18th century Liverpool employed more than one half of the vessels involved in slavery and imported annually from Africa more than one half of slaves purchased by all vessels in the whole of Great Britain. The number of clearances from Liverpool to Africa in subsequent years continued to grow (see Table 1 in Part 2). So that by the 1780s there were nearly twice as many slaving vessels clearing from Liverpool as there were from London and Bristol combined.

"Three out of every four slaves shipped to Jamaica between 1761 and 1771 were carried on Liverpool ships, and all but three of the 19 most important British firms engaged in slave trading were based in Liverpool." Cameron & Cooke (ibid).

So firm a grip of control did Liverpool have over the trade in slaves that by the close of the 18th century it is estimated that 60% of all British slave trading activities, which represented a 40% control of slave trading in Europe, centred on the city. It is not difficult to see the appropriateness of the title capital of the slave trade: it described 18th century Liverpool very accurately.

Liverpool was the last British city to be directly involved in the slave trade, slow to become involved and even slower to relinquish its source of economic power. It kept its firm grip on the trade until the last possible moment. By 1800 Cameron and Cooke describe Liverpool's control as *"invincible"*. Between January 1806 and the abolition of the slave trade in May of the following year 185 slavers cleared from Liverpool and carried with them nearly 50,000 Africans to slavery in the Americas.

It has been estimated that Liverpool's net proceeds from the entire African trade in 1783-93 were £12,294,116; or £117,647 per year, for each successive year (4). This profit was accrued on the basis of 878 voyages, and the sale of 303,737 slaves. A considerable proportion of the profit was returned to a relatively small number of prominant Liverpool men, men who had both political and economic power.

THE SLAVE TRADERS

Thomas Johnson who was Mayor of Liverpool in 1695, sat as MP from 1701 to 1723, was knighted in 1708 and was described as *"the founder of the modern town of Liverpool"*. He was also part owner of the slaving ship 'Blessing'. Both Sir Thomas Street and Johnson Street are named after him. A number of other 'sons of the city', whose names streets and other institutions still remember, boasted both political and economic power in the city and direct involvement in the slave trade. These include: **Richard Gildart**, Mayor in 1714, 1731 and 1736 and MP for Liverpool 1734-54; **Foster Cunliffe** who became Liverpool's leading merchant (perhaps the biggest 'businessman' in the whole country). Cunliffe was Mayor of Liverpool in 1716, 1729 and 1735. He was also part-owner of at least four slavers, one of which he named after himself, 'Foster'. Altogether these ships held 1,120 slaves, and they brought the Cunliffe family enough profit to load a dozen ships a year with sugar and rum for sale in England.

Most of the profits from the slave trade were channelled into banking: the best example of this is with the **Heywood** family. The Heywood brothers, having made their fortunes from slavery, and having married rich heiresses, became bankers. The Heywood banking legacy continued up until 1883 when it was absorbed by Martin's Bank which in turn was absorbed by Barclays Bank. There still remains a Heywoods branch of Barclay's in Victoria Street Liverpool.

By 1750, 10 of Liverpool's 14 most prominent banks were owned by slave traders. The traders then being in a position to both finance and insure their own private ventures, as well as those of others. Further, by 1787, 37 of the 41 members of the Liverpool council were involved, in one way or another, in slavery, as were all of Liverpool's 20 Lord Mayors who held office between 1787 and 1807. One of the huge bronze plaques which dominate the Liverpool Town Hall's main committee room is engraved with their names.

As well as self-made men such as joiners and ship-builders, some of whom made fortunes from the slave trade, some of Liverpool's older and more respected families were *"more or less, steeped in slavery." Fryer (ibid).*

John Gladstone was an absent landlord whose family profited from the sale of sugar and rum produced by slaves in British Guyana and Jamaica. (His son William Gladstone later became a Liberal Prime Minister). As a Conservative Member of Parliament he defended slavery in the Caribbean arguing that emancipation would not be in the best interest of slaves.

Slavery in Liverpool was carried out *"..with vitality that was worthy of a better cause"* (5). This trade in human lives was not seen as problematic , it was seen as an effective way to maximise profit. Once there was an ideology in place which was able to appease the consciences of those involved, the race was on to make as much money as possible, and as quickly as possible. Slave sales in Liverpool, slave ships, merchants and bankers only tell part of the story of slavery, but an integral part which forms one side of the triangular trade. Dicky Sam says of slavery in Liverpool that:

"...... time, money, and thought all brought so powerfully into play, that it ought to have shocked humanity, and been a perpetual disgrace to a barbarous people, and how much more to a civilized community, and a people professing Christianity. But then, slavery was right; it was supported by the bible, and strenuously advocated by the clergy of the time, as well as politicians."

LEARNING OUTCOMES

a) Pupils and students will be aware of the fact that slave trading and the owning of slaves, was seen as an acceptable, and respectable, economic venture in Liverpool in the 18th and 19th centuries.

b) Pupils and students will be aware that Lord Mayors, bankers and Members of Parliament were directly involved in slave trading, and that they were well placed to facilitate their own interests.

c) To expose the true relationship between slavery and the economic development of Liverpool. Through a close reading of the materials presented in Part Two pupils and students will be able to enter into the debate about the extent to which slavery was the economic foundation upon which Britain's industry was built.

d) To show, through documentary evidence, that Liverpool was directly involved in slavery prior to 1760.

NATIONAL CURRICULUM

Through class room activities, exercises and teacher led discussion pupils and students will:

A) understand that there is more than one interpretation of an historical fact.

B) have some understanding of how historical events come to bear on the lives of people today.

C) be aware of the fact that the physical environment of Liverpool holds a number of 'clues' about its past, particularly in its architecture and in its street names. (also in the dock area).

D) be able to draw conclusions from primary and secondary source materials and develop skills in order to make critical analysis.

Background image: Slaves marching to the coast of African for transportation to America and the Caribbean

REFERENCES

(1) **Gall Cameron & Stan Cooke** *'Liverpool Capital Of The Slave Trade.'* Picton Press Ltd. 1992.

(2) **Peter Fryer** *'Staying Power - The History Of Black People In Britain'.* Pluto Press 1983.

(3) **From the Liverpool Maritime Museum** *Exhibition On Slavery.*

(4) **Gomer Williams** *'The Liverpool Privateers - with An Account Of The Liverpool Slave Trade.'* Heinemann 1897.

(5) **Dicky Sam** *'Liverpool And The Slave Trade.'* Scouse Press - First Published in 1884. Centenary Edition published in 1984.

Sir Thomas Johnson
'Pioneering' Liverpool Slave Trader

THE ABOLITION OF

SLAVERY

INTRODUCTION

There are three schools of thought in contention as to the reasons for the abolition of slavery. There is the partial history of the Abolitionist Movement with attention directed to the development of the moral character of the Parliamentary struggle. Against this is usually pitted the case of economic decline, and the assertion of new economic interests making abolition, in some sense, inevitable and slavery unsustainable. Latterly there has been the recognition of the Black Abolitionists who are not often considered from the point of view of how they impacted upon each contending view but solely as a 'stand alone' history. All standpoints will be examined in turn, though the intention here is to focus on the Black Abolitionists and indicate pointers to a more integrated account of the abolition of slavery.

THE MORAL CASE: A CASE FOR SELF GLORIFICATION?

"The British people may take credit for bringing about abolition at considerable expense to themselves and then enforcing it single handed among Africans and Arabs, who believed it to be the normal way of life.... more than anything else this was due to the work of three men, Granville Sharpe, Thomas Clarkson and William Wilberforce." Ransford, 'The Slave Trade' 1971 (1).

Sharpe, Clarkson and Wilberforce were members of the Abolition Society formed in 1787. The work of these individuals usually looms large in most treatments of reasons for the abolition of the slave trade. Thomas Clarkson's place in the movement is pinned to his accumulation of evidence for presentation to Parliament and two works : *'Essays On Slavery and Commerce of Human Species'.*(2) (which won Cambridge Universities Senior Latin Prize and was translated into English in 1786), and *'History on the Abolition of the Slave Trade.'* which he published in 1808. (3)

The historical evidence indicates that Clarkson was a more radical campaigner than Wilberforce, but it is Wilberforce who is more often recognised because he was an M.P. and this put him in the position of being the parliamentary spokesperson for the campaign. Having the ear of the Prime Minister Pitt as a personal friend helped to secure his prominence. Granville Sharp is largely remembered for bringing the **Somerset Case** to court and winning it in 1772. Somerset was an enslaved African who escaped from the Caribbean to England. The Somerset Case established that a slave once arrived in England was a free person. 15,000 slaves in England are said to have been freed by this case.

To understand more fully the part that these people played in the abolition of slavery it is necessary to look to the intellectual foundations of the movement they belonged to. Quakers like John Woolman saw moral corruption of young apprentice sailors on slave ships. Methodists like John Wesley saw Britain as stained with *"blood and guilt"*, and in danger of divine retribution. Daniel Defoe's *'Robinson Crusoe'* depicted the African as the saviour of the white man. Adam Smith made the economic case in terms of the slaves' lack of motivation towards a system which gave nothing back; and ways in which the relationship of favoured trading with colonies stopped goods being obtained cheaper elsewhere. Thus a whole range of interests could and were mobilised.

Perhaps James Tobin writing in support of West India Interest for the Monthly Review in 1786, adequately sums up what the stakes in the lust for glory were....

"to take down such a gigantic mass of deformity by gradual efforts would undoubtedly immortalise the genius who would complete such a work." (4)

This view of England and the prominent role the leading abolitionists gave to themselves came under severe attack from the Caribbean historian Eric Williams:

"The abolitionist role has been seriously misunderstood and greatly exaggerated. When British merchants depended on the West Indies they ignored slavery or defended it. When they found the West Indian Sugar Industry had become a nuisance they destroyed slavery. This would lead to the end of West Indian control of the Sugar Industry. What really counted were the forces of economic and not "moral" change. The abolitionists' role insofar as they had one was to help the process along." (5)

Certainly there is a lot of evidence to support Williams' case. From the 1790s the price of sugar from the French Colonies was 20% lower than the British, and French exports to European markets outstripped Britain's. Some merchants had already begun to move out of sugar production and had become, or joined up with, industrialists. In addition industrial, manufacturing and commerical interests had begun to assert themselves. Those interests that once formed a powerful lobby in Parliament were in decline and would inevitably be defeated. Making this case does not belittle the modern campaigning methods, such as the boycott and pamphleteering, which the movement bequeathed to us as an expression of the power in the industrial age that could be used to mobilise people in their hundreds and thousands. More so it is to put it in its proper place.

PROFITS ARE MADE BY PEOPLE: THE SYSTEM IS UNWORKABLE

The views of Ransford and Williams are to be contrasted with those of historians like James who was concerned to make human activity central to the writing of history. His book, 'The Black Jacobins', is a demonstration of the taking of destiny into ones own hands. Under the leadership of Toussaint L' Ouverture the enslaved Africans of Haiti fought and defeated the French army to make the only completely successful slave revolution.

The idea of self representation is one of the most important features of the Abolitionist Movement. It is what put Black Abolitionists onto the map and helps recast perspectives. It is a good starting point for understanding the world in which people like Wilberforce moved.

Those monumental Black Abolitionists whose names have a certain common currency is the place to begin. Oluadah Equiano, who bought his freedom from his master and lived in Britain, Frederick Douglas and Sojouner Truth who escaped to freedom from slavery in America are to be our main figures.

Olaudah Equiano is included here because he was one of the few free Black people in Britain active and writing in the 1780s for whom we have a direct record.

On the question of self representation, Douglas experienced it like this:

"I felt strongly moved to speak...(but) the truth was I felt myself a slave, and the idea of speaking to white people weighted me down. Then I spoke but a few moments, when I felt a considerable degree of freedom and said what I desired with considerable ease." (6)

The issue of Black people speaking about their experiences made a big impact on the development of the Abolitionist Movement. It brought out a moral authority that could not be raised otherwise. This is how Sojourner Truth saw it:

"The Lord gave me the name Sojourner because I was to travel up and down the land showing people their sins and being a sign to them. Afterwards I told the Lord I wanted another name.... and the Lord gave me Truth, because I was to declare the truth unto the people." (7)

On the question of slavery and its abolition Equiano had this to say:

"Sometimes indeed we sold slaves to them (Europeans) but they were only prisoners of war or such among us as had been convicted of kidnapping or adultery

a crime which we esteemed heinous. This practice of kidnapping induces me to think, that not withstanding our strictness, their principal business among us was to trepam our people."(8)

On the barbarities and iniquities of slavery, Equiano had this to say:

"Indeed on the most trifling occasion they were loaded with chains and often instruments of torture were added. The iron muzzle, thumb screw etc... were sometimes applied for the slightest fault." Equiano (ibid).

RECASTING THE ROLE OF THE ABOLITIONISTS

Indeed it is in this role and beyond that the work of white Abolitionists must be judged. Equiano assisted Granville Sharpe in the development of the struggle against slavery. He brought to his attention slaves in need of help and gave evidence for submission to parliamentary matters pertaining to the slave trade and was consulted by Prime Minister Pitt about it. When seen from this standpoint we must also see the case of Somerset from another point of view.

To state the obvious, without Somerset's willingness to fight for freedom through the courts, there would be no case. In fact it was the self example which mobilised others.It has been observed:

"After the Somerset Case, slaves began to try to free themselves to exploit the law to their own advantage."(9). But nothing is said of the moving figure for the inspiration.

Black Abolitionists like Douglas understood that for the credibility of this movement amongst Black people, they had to be seen to take the lead in many spheres:

"Our Present position at the Head of an Anti-Slavery Journal, has resulted from no unworthy distrust or ungrateful want of appreciation... of the noble band of White Labourers.... but from the sincere and settled conviction that such a journal if conducted with only moderate skill and ability, would do a most important and indispen-

sable work, which it would be wholly impossible for our white friends to do for you." (10).

The Black Abolitionists concerns often did not stop at their own condition, but were part of and contributed to the general issues of the day from the standpoint of their own experiences. Olaudah Equiano is known to have attended gatherings on radical platforms to speak out against slavery, and we can be sure he was acquainted with other cases and causes. Perhaps one of the most haunting examples of this is to be found in Sojouner Truth's address to the Women's Convention in Ohio in 1851:

Ain't I A Woman

That man over there say a woman needs to be helped into carriages and lifted over ditches and to have the best place ever. Nobody ever helped me into carriages or over mud puddles or give me a best place.

That little man in black there say a woman can't have as much rights a man cause Christ wasn't a woman. Where did your Christ come from? From God and a woman! Man had nothing to do with him! If the first woman God ever made was strong enough to turn the world upside down all along to - gether women ought to be able to turn it rightside up again. Taken from 'Daughters of Africa.'(11)

As in any movement there are strains, tensions and conflicts as to the best path to pursue to freedom. It is not without irony that one of Olaudah Equiano's most celebrated acts came effectively when he was acting as a Commissary of Provisions and Stores on board a ship transporting Black people to Sierra Leone in Africa. On discovering that the white agent was selling the provisions and pocketing the profits Equiano reported him to the authorities and for this he was sacked.

Household names in the ranks of Black Abolitionists have often flirted with this issue of return or repatriation, Henry Highland Garnet saw it this way:

"I hesitate not to say that my mind of late has greatly changed in regard to the American colonisation scheme.... I would rather see a man free in Liberia than a slave in the United States." 'African In America' (ibid).

Despite holding different opinions it was possible for people like Garnet and Douglas to participate in networks such as the underground rail road which smuggled slaves from slave holding states to non slave holding states.

NO WAY OUT: UNITY UNDER PRESSURE

What seems to have determined their attitude was the degree or lack of progress being made in the struggle for freedom and the fact that some issues were more decisive than others. For a time pro and anti violence factions in the movement seemed irreconcilable. The crystalising moment for many factions came around 'The Dread Scott Judgment' of 1857. A Supreme court judgment ruled that Negroes could not bring a suit in Federal Court because they *"could not be citizens of the United States"*. Prior to this Douglas held the view that freedom could be obtained by agitation:

"Be resolved that in the language of inspired wisdom there shall be no peace to the wicked, and that this guilty nation shall have no peace, and that we will do all we can to agitate! Agitate!! AGITATE!!! till our rights are restored and our brethren are redeemed from their cruel chains." Douglas (ibid)

A VOICE FROM THE PAST

From the beginning people like Garnet had begun to question this policy. Taking his cue from David Walker, who, writing in the year 1830, one year before the revolt of Nat Turner, the leader of an unsuccessful slave uprising, in

opposition to Douglas' School of Thought counselled:

"Let your motto be Resistance! Resistance ! Resistance! No Oppressed people have ever secured their liberty without resistance..... Trust in the living god..... and remember that you are three millions." (12).

FIGHT TO THE FINISH!

At the 1843 Negro Convention in Buffalo New York this motion was narrowly defeated by one vote. With a host of examples of the direct action of San Domingo before them Garnet knew he was treading on fertile ground. Assessing the impact of the rebellion in Montego Bay in Jamaica led by the Baptist lay preacher Sam "Daddy" Sharpe Rev Henry Bleby noted,

"The revolt failed of accomplishing the immediate purpose, yet by it a further wound was delivered to slavery, which accelerated its destruction for it demonstrated to the imperial legislature that among the Negroes themselves the spirit of freedom had been so widely diffused as to render it most perilous to postpone the settlement of the most important question of emancipation to a later period."
Reproduced in Hart (ibid)

The rebels had caused £1.5 million worth of damage. In effect, Garnet called on people to carry on doing what they had done, but to make it more widespread.

Cast into depths of despair by the refusal of slave holding states to join the Union and give up slavery, Douglas abandoned the pacifist stance he had taken 6 months earlier:

"....the sable arms which have been engaged in beautifying and adorning the south were engaged in spreading death and devastation there." Douglas (ibid)

The mood in the Black Community was swinging full circle. The Free Black people in the North found they were making little progress. This is exemplified in the commonly held view put forward by Charles McKay. He put it thus:

"We shall not make the black man a slave we shall not buy him or sell him;...but he shall not be free to dine and drink at our board - to plead in our courts - to represent us in the legislature..... He is inferior. Let him know his place and keep it."
African Americans (ibid).

This situation is a metaphor for the post slavery situation in the Caribbean. The influx of European migrants into the north intensified this situation. The Fugitive Slave Act of 1850 allowing any African American to be taken out of their home and returned to bondage without resort to law engulfed both the Northern and Southern Black communities. Black people mobilised to protect themselves. The Dread Scott Judgement removed the doubts that lingered.

AFRICANS FIGHT AGAINST SLAVERY - THE MAKING OF A NATION

In 1854 Delaney had correctly prophesised:

"the great issue sooner or later upon which must be disputed the world's destiny, will be the question of black and white, and every individual will be called upon for his identity with one or the other." (13)

The world the slaves made had reached a cross roads. The North wanted the slaves labour for the development of industry, the South wanted to maintain the control of this labour and to preserve the dominance of agriculture. At the same time these states were entering into a political union where the issue was one of who would form the legislation for the land. This was to be settled by war and the question of whose side Black people fought on proved decisive.

Delaney, who had been planing to raise an African Cavalry to fight for freedom, joined the union to become the first African Captain in the U.S. Army. Douglas, who had been making plans to leave for Haiti, encouraged his sons and others to enlist in the Union Army.

CONCLUSION:

WHAT COULD BE DONE?

Clearly a full account of the history of the Abolitionist Movement cannot be written from just one standpoint. Our reflections on the actions of the Black Abolitionists should also make us stop and think about the actions of people like Wilberforce. It is simply not good enough to argue for history based on people's actions and in the same breath dismiss them with the economic arguments of Eric Williams. Equally the Williams view fails to take into account the slaves' aim of making the system of the organisation of production unworkable. In this connection Fryer's estimation that every two years there was a revolt somewhere shows something of the rate of destruction being inflicted in the Caribbean. In this way individual action cannot be seperated from economic activities.

The Black Abolitionist's motivation towards the destruction of production based on slavery is unquestionable. In many ways that has been the main point; but it needs to be set in context if its to be properly understood. From the wars against slavery in Africa, to the suicides on board ship, through to the insurrection on the Amistad, the community of exslaves in Palmares in Brazil, down to the short lived guerilla war led by people such as Nanny of the Maroons, through to the Haitian Revolution, there is need for perspective. In other words, if the opportunities for rebellion or revolution are few, then acts of resistance or use of legal means for progress are likely to follow. However, where there are pressures for open revolt and there is a chance for success then each climatic challenge can make for the movement from resistance to revolt to revolution. These changes as a process feed upon each other. This can be seen as an explanation for the difference between what happened in the Caribbean, where slaves were in the majority, in America where slaves were in a few states; and in England where they were either isolated in small pockets, or formed a part of small communities in the major cities.

LEARNING OUTCOMES

(a) Pupils and students through a close study of primary and secondary source materials in Part Two, and through further research, will be aware that there is more than one way of viewing the abolition of the slave trade.

(b) Pupils and students will understand the important role that Black people played in the abolition of the Slave Trade. They will be able to name Black abolitionists, be aware of what their contribution was to the abolition and be able to detail aspects of their work and life.

(c) Pupils and students will be able to name female abolitionists and be able to say something about their lives and work.

(d) Pupils and students will be aware of how Black people made the system of slavery unworkable, not only by speaking out against the trade and making pubic its evils, but through rebellions in the Caribbean, through uprisings on ships, through running away and through putting the spanner in the works of agricultural production on the plantations.

(e) Through further research pupils and students should be able to find out more about:

* the American Civil War and the role that Black people played in it - pupils and students should understand the significance of this war as it relates to the emancipation of Black people in America;

* legal cases which aimed to establish the position of Black people in various countries (America, the Caribbean and Britain).

NATIONAL CURRICULUM

(A) Pupils and students will be able to improve their analytical powers and their powers of evaluation; and draw conclusions based on evidence through a reading of the exercises in Part Two.

(B) Pupils and students will gain an insight and begin to develop an empathy and understanding of the experiences and motivation of the Black Abolitionists.

(C) Pupils and students should further develop their understanding of how the system of slavery contributed to the economic development of Britain and the effect that the abolition of slavery had on the British economy. They will begin to discuss and further understand the nature of industrialisation and the system of capitalism which came out of slavery.

REFERENCES

(1)   **Oliver Ransford** *'The Slave Trade'* Published in 1971.

(2)   **Thomas Clarkeson** *'Essays On Slavery And The Commerce Of The Human Species.'* - Written in 1786.

(3)   *'A History Of The Abolition Of The Slave Trade'* 1808.

(4)   **Richard Hart** *'Slaves Who Abolished Slavery'*. Vol 1. Published by the Institute of Social and Economic Research, the University of the West Indies.

(5)   **Eric Williams** *'Capitalism and Slavery'*. Andre Deutsch 1964.

(6)   **Fredrick Douglas** *'The Life And Times Of Fredrick Douglas'*. Pub by Macmillan, New York 1962.

(7)   *'African Americans'*. Published by W.G.B.H Boston. History Unit 1993.

(8)   **Olaudah Equiano** *'Equiano's Travels'* Edited by Paul Edwards. Published by Longman's 1984.

(9)   *'A History Of The Black Presence In London'* Produced by the **London Strategic Policy Unit** / Greater London Council 1986.

(10)   **Joanne Grant (Ed)** ' *Black Protest: History, Documents & Analysis; 1619 To The Present'*. Fawcett Publications.

(11)   **Margaret Bushby** *'Daughters Of Africa'*. Published by Vintage 1993.

(12)   **Tomas. R. Frazier** *'Afro American History: Primary Sources'*. Publishers, New York, Harcourt, Brace and Javanovich - 1971

(13) **Dorothy Sterling** *'The Making of An Afro-American: Martin Robinson Delaney 1812-1885'* New York, Doubleday 1971.

Frederick Douglas, one of the abolitionist movements most effective orators.
By Elisha Hammond

BLACK RESISTANCE AND REBELLION

INTRODUCTION

The history of the African diaspora during the period under discussion, the period of modern slavery, has been one of resilience and resistance. It is one that has been characterised by individual achievement, in the face of the most horrific adversities, and individual and collective struggles for liberty and equality.

We have already looked at the role of Black Abolitionists such as Olaudah Equiano and Sojouner Truth, whose contributions must take centre stage and be given the true recognition that they are deserving of. In this section we look at specific examples of how Black people made slavery unworkable in the Caribbean and the Americas through rebellion and through sabotaging the system of production in, for example, the plantations. We also look at the ingenious ways in which Black people helped each other to win their freedom, for example through the 'underground railroad', and through the development of chants, songs, language and culture, all of which signalled the way to freedom.

C.L.R. James (1) says of Black people in the Caribbean during the period of the British occupation that,

> " the difficulty was that though one could trap them (Africans) like animals, transport them in pens, work them alongside an ass or a horse and beat them both with the same stick, stable them and starve them, they remained, despite their black skin and curly hair, quite invincibly human beings with a thirst for liberation and the strength of conviction to achieve it."

Slavery was legally ended throughout the British Empire on 1 August 1834. As a system of production it was becoming increasingly unprofitable. There was a strong Abolitionist Movement, a more profitable economic system about to supersede slavery and there were middle-class humanitarians and working-class movements speaking out against it. But, above all, "...*the Caribbean was seething with unrest.*" (2) and as Fryer notes:

> "*A black revolution throughout the British West Indies, designed to abolish slavery from below, was 'widely apprehended', both in the West Indies and in Britain. And it was in fact the Jamaican uprising of 1831-32, the so-called 'Baptist War', that proved the decisive factor precipitating emancipation.*"

From the introduction of slavery into the Caribbean at the beginning of the 16th century, the white planters and colonists lived in constant fear of slave revolts. As Ferguson (3), informs us armed uprisings occurred frequently, particularly in the 18th century, when the slave population was at its highest. Revolts were crushed by colonial militias, who, as Douglas (4) informs us, "*were neither well equipped with arms nor was their discipline good*", but this did not deter the slaves whose only means to freedom was to either revolt, run away or sabotage production in the plantations.

SAN DOMINGUE

The most famous slave revolt started in 1791 in the French colony of San Domingue, which became the so-called 'Negro State of Haiti'. In 1789 the colony of San Domingue supplied two thirds of the overseas trade of France and was the greatest individual market for the slave trade. As James states,

> "*it was the greatest individual market for the European slave trade. It was an integral part of the economic life of the age, the greatest colony in the world, the prize of France and the envy of every other imperialist nation.*" (ibid)

However, in 1789 the French Revolution began with its battle cry of "*Liberty, Equality, Fraternity.*" This cry was heard in the French colonies in which liberty, equality and fraternity did not exist. As in other European colonies in the West Indies in San Domingue there were a number of distinct social groups, a hierarchy which was rigidly defined in terms of skin colouration. There were the wealthy and powerful whites, the *"grands blancs"*, there were the free people of colour, at the time described as coloureds, free Blacks and slaves. The freed coloureds and Blacks were not in a position to enjoy the same opportunities or have the same rights as their white counterparts. Similarly there were some educated and relatively wealthy coloureds who, socially and economically speaking, were in a better position than some poor whites

When the French revolution began these economic, political and social differences were to be the focus upon which the San Domingue revolution would be set; with the liberty and equality of Black people taking centre stage. Douglas (ibid) sums up the impetus for the revolution thus:

> *"In 1791 the revolutionary government in France announced that in the French colonies coloured people born of free parents should have equal political rights as whites. The whites in St. Domingue refused to accept this, and fighting began between whites and freed coloureds. Then, as whites and coloureds were fighting it out, the slaves revolted."*

This became a long-standing struggle for freedom in which the slaves of San Domingue began to rely on the leadership of Toussaint L'Ouverture. In Part Two we look more closely at the detail of the San Domingue revolutions and the impact it had on slavery in the Caribbean.

THE MAROONS

There were then many escapes and uprisings in the Caribbean. In fact it would be accurate to say that such escapes and uprisings were characteristic of the Caribbean during slavery and, as we have seen, eventually made the system unsustainable. From when the British first took Jamaica from the Spanish they were plagued with difficulties. What Robinson describes as, *"the first big recorded slave outbreak"* (5) took place in 1684. It was not, however, until 1690 that *"a really dangerous insurrection occurred"*. This took place near Chapeltown in the parish of Clarendon and was

probably started due to brutal treatment towards slaves. The slaves killed the plantation overseer and seized arms and ammunition. Although some of the slaves were captured the next day, many of them managed to escape into the hills. It is believed that among those who managed to escape was a slave named Cudjoe. The runaways settled in the Clarendon Hills.

At this time there were already settlements formed in the north east of the island. They were occupied by what became know as the Maroons. They provided a refuge for runaways who, on leaving the plantations, would make their way to what they believed was a sanctuary from slavery. Cudjoe did not form part of the established group but rather formed his own Maroons. His, and other, small groups began raiding the farms of the settlers in the more remote parts of the island. In this way they made life difficult for settlers on the one hand, whilst providing an alternative way of life for slaves on the other. There is evidence that the Maroons kept in regular contact with slaves on farms and plantations. Robinson *(ibid)* describes the way in which the Maroons operated:

> *"The Clarendon gangs kept in constant touch with the slaves on the plantations, many of whom were old friends or even relatives. In lean times they were often supplied with food from the provision grounds of the slaves and occasionally some of the bolder slaves joined their ranks. One result of this constant communication was that the runaways could usually be warned whenever armed parties of militia or soldiers were moving against them. At first the small raiding parties of the Clarendon runaways were content to kill cattle, but gradually their raids became more formidable. They plundered the houses of the more isolated settlers, destroyed or drove away their cattle and carried off their slaves. They so harassed the country round about their hideouts that the development of that particular part of Jamaica was greatly retarded."*

In time many of the runaway gangs joined forces, and merged together to form a single unit. Cudjoe became the leader of all of the Maroons and in time they become involved in a more *"regular and* "connected system of warfare" against solders, the militias and armed detachments of American Indians bought from the Mosquito Coast by the Government which had decided to take positive action against the Maroons. The first struggle with the Maroons was to last for more than forty years and during that time forty four Acts were passed by the Assembly in its attempts to suppress the Maroons. It is also estimated that £240, 000 was spent in the same endeavour, but to the same effect. It would not be until 1734 that any real success was achieved in the battle against the Maroons. In that year Nanny Town, the stronghold of the Eastern Maroons, was destroyed.

PLANTATION SOCIETY

No one opposed slavery more than the slaves themselves. There are countless examples of the extraordinary actions and determination of those who refused to accept the status of a slave. New slaves, on arrival in the Caribbean, refused to work in the plantations and refused to answer to the new names given to them by their new 'owners'. There are memorable sections from Alex Haley's *'Roots'* (6) which detail such determination to maintain a sense of dignity and pride in an alien and hostile land, and maintain the last vestige of culture and identity, one's name.

Suicide was a common form of protest, particularly among those who had recently arrived, having been stolen from their tribes and sold, suffered the great wait in the compounds for a full 'compliment' , having gone through the Middle Passage only to be sold again on arrival in the Caribbean and put to work. Those slaves who had become familiar with how plantation society worked had their own forms of protest. They purposely worked slowly, they damaged tools, they pretended to be ill, wounded themselves and poisoned estate animals. There are also accounts of slaves poisoning overseers and of so-called 'nannys' poisoning babies. Such action ground down production and made plantocratic societies less than attractive. It is largely for this reason that as soon as plantation owners could afford to they would go back to England, leaving their business concerns in the hands of overseers:

Claypole and Robottom (7) inform us that owners and overseers feared poisoning by their slaves almost as much as they feared rebellion,

"Poison was suspected whenever a white overseer died suddenly, although the cause was more likely to be heavy drinking or poor medical care."

Slaves of African birth were aware of their white masters' ignorance of African languages, places and customs. The use of African language was difficult to preserve, particularly because slave catchers in Africa were careful to separate those who were likely to collude together and plan to escape. At each stage of the Triangular Trade there was scope to separate those who spoke the same languages and who shared the same culture. And, as stated, slaves could be further isolated and prevented from communicating in African languages when sold to estates and plantations in the Caribbean. Despite this, African languages, religions, music, folk-lore and dances persisted. This provided the slaves not only with a means of escape, but with the necessary implements for maintaining their cultural identity and sabotaging plantocratic society.

ESCAPEES AND FREE MEN

The vast majority of slaves, as we have shown, found ways to rebel, or found ways of making plantation society problematic for owners. Some slaves committed suicide on board slaving ships, but most either found ways of making their existence as slaves tolerable, or devised the means for their escape. Slaves would often find ingenious ways, not only of facilitating their own escape, but facilitating the escape of others . American slaves, for example, found ingenious ways of passing on messages through their songs, the so-called 'Negro Spirituals', many of which contained coded messages known only to other slaves. One such song was called, *'Follow The Drinking Gourd'*. The Drinking Gourd was the American name for the constellation known in England as *'The Plough'*.

At a particular time of the year the Drinking Gourd can be seen in the Northern sky. As Canada, which abolished slavery before America, lies to the north of the United States, when slaves wanted to escape they would travel by night using the stars as their compass to the north. Another song used to transfer coded messages was *'Swing Low, Sweet*

Chariots'. This song contains the following lines: *"...a band of angels coming after me, coming for to carry me home."* Sometimes slaves on the run would seek shelter in dockland areas, they would try to find work and mingle amongst the busy crowds working as labourers loading and unloading ships. The song *'Swing Low, Sweet Chariots'* would be sung by fellow slaves to warn an escaped slave that their owner's gang was in the area, usually accompanied by dogs, to hunt down their master's 'property'. Although the word 'angels' was used as a code word for the slave-hunters, they never were.

American slaves who had managed to free themselves in one way or another were often anxious to make known the plight of their fellows and would travel around Britain, in much the same way as Olaudah Equiano had done earlier. The main forum in England was Exeter Hall which was run by the British and Foreign Anti-Slavery lobby. Smaller 'Exeter Halls' sprang up all over the country, built by socialists in the 1840s. Liverpool had its own Exeter Hall. Located in Lord Nelson Street near the main area of Black settlement, it was the largest of the halls. Many Black ex-slave lecturers visiting Liverpool were given the opportunity of providing educational programmes illustrating everyday life in the plantations. This lectures often detailed escapes.

One of the most well known of those to pass through Exeter Hall was William Wells Brown a Black American. Arriving in Europe in 1849 Wells spent five years in Britain, during which time he spoke at one thousand meetings to plead the cause of Black people still held in bondage, as slavery was not to be abolished in America until 1865.

Individual Black slaves struggled to keep their dignity in the face of almost impossible odds. As mentioned earlier, Black slaves who spoke the same language were not allowed to remain together, family life and emotional ties were forbidden, the slaves' own culture was forbidden, their own religions were banned. Any form of education of the slaves was discouraged and often owners liked to mock their slaves by calling them names usually given to dogs, or to Greek gods and mythological characters. In this way their real African names were ignored.

One slave who managed to record how he suffered was the West African Muslim named Ayuda Suleiman Diallo, known in England as Job Ben Solomon. Ayuba had been captured as a slave and sold to an English sea captain. The captain had been so impressed with Ayuba's ability to write the entire Koran from memory that he publicised the fact. Ayuba was soon admitted into learned circles in England, but not before a letter, written in Arabic by his father, had so touched his owner when translated by an Oxford professor that he was given his freedom in 1734. During his stay in England he was befriended by the Duke of Montagu. His frequent visits to the Duke's house were not liked by the servants, who complained that he soiled the stairs by retiring so often to his room to pray.

A similar story is that of the slave known to us simply as 'Mohammed', another Muslim slave of a planter in the Caribbean island of Antigua at the end of the 18th century. Extremely well versed in Arabic literature, this devout young man was eventually given his freedom in much the same way as Ayuba Suleiman Diallo. The fact that he chose to come to Liverpool in 1811 may have been prompted by the knowledge of the growing free Black population there at the time.

It must be understood that these slaves were fortunate in both being set free and being in a position to have their story passed down to us. Most slaves were forced to live out their entire lives with no hope of freedom and in appalling conditions. Ayuba's story nevertheless provides us with a rare glimpse of the life of a free African in Britain in the 19th century. It also provides us with a common picture of resilience, one characteristic of the African diaspora.

LEARNING OUTCOMES

a) Pupils and students will be aware of the role that Black people played in their own liberation slavery. It is particularly important for them to understand how this role manifested itself in Africa, during the Middle Passage, in the Caribbean, America and in England.

b) Through a close reading of primary and secondary source materials in Part Two, pupils and students will be able to detail the ways in which Black people made the system of slavery unworkable. They should be aware of the importance of rebellions in the Caribbean and be able to detail at least one of them.

c) Pupils and students should be in a position to assess the effect of ideas and events in Europe on the lives of people in the Caribbean and mainland America.

d) Pupils and students will understand, and be able to give examples of, how African culture, language, music etc., were used as the necessary implements of sabotage in plantocratic society.

NATIONAL CURRICULUM

(A) Pupils and students through a close reading of activities and exercises in Part Two will understand how individuals can emerge as historically significant figures - Toussaint L'Ouverature for example. They will also be aware of collective action as in the activities of the Maroons.

(B) Pupils and students will be able to reach logical conclusions from primary and second source materials. This is particularly important in contrasting the standard explanations for the abolition of the slave trade, the abolitionists, with the actions of individuals.

(C) Pupils and students will develop their analytical skills, particularly through research. They should be encouraged to find out more information in relation to the economic argument put forward to explain the abolition of slavery.

(D) Pupils and students should be encouraged to explore the issues of the abolition of slavery as a cross-curricular theme.

(E) Pupils and students should be encouraged to do project work on the Maroons, finding out more information about their activities.

REFERENCES

(1) **CLR James** *'The Black Jacobins -Toussaint L' Ouverture And The San Domingo Revolution'*. Virgin Publishing 1938.

(2) **Peter Fryer** *'Black People In The British Empire'*. Pluto Press 1984.

(3) **James Ferguson** *'Far From Paradise'*. The Latin American Bureau 1990.

(4) **Douglas Hall** *'The Caribbean Experience - An Historic Survey 1450 -1960'*. Heinemann Educational Books 1982.

(5) **Robinson.** Reproduced in Hall (ibid).

(6) **Alex Haley** *'Roots'*. Published by Vintage 1991.

(7) **William Claypole & John Robottom** *'Caribbean Story'*. Longman Caribbean 1986.

Image: Impression of the St. Domingue Revolution. In 1773 Slaves led by Toussaint L'Ouverture defeated plantation owners and set up and independent state.

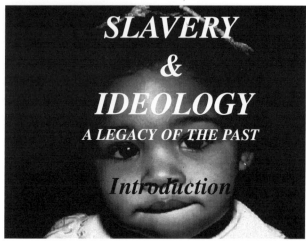

There can be no doubt that slavery as an institution would not have been possible without an ideology which could justify it. It would have been impossible for Europeans to enslave African people unless there was a way of sanctioning what was a brutal and murderous trade in human lives. Slavery was made workable by first reducing those who were to be enslaved to a subspecies, to something less than human. Christopher Columbus, for example, was able to treat native American Indians, and later Africans, in a savage way because he believed them to be less than human. They had a very different religion to the Spanish, their culture and language differed, and what's more, they were not Christian. They were considered to be heathens and therefore less than human. Once this construction had been created, it became possible to treat both Amerindians and Africans in a brutal manner; Europeans being secure in the knowledge that God was on their side and that their newly enslaved peoples could serve as a useful means to a profitable economic end. If some could be converted to Christianity along the way then this would be in keeping with the mission of Christians.

The reality of slavery was that very few people were converted to Christianity (1). Not only was this unworkable, but it was not particularly desirable. However, Christopher Columbus managed to convince Queen Isabella and King Ferdinand that he had converted many native Amerindians. The main aim of slavery was to capture labour and to squeeze as much energy out of that labour as possible whilst expending the minimum of energy necessary in order to make that labour both functional and profitable.

In the final section of *'An Introduction To The African Holocaust'* we look at slavery ideology, propaganda and popular perceptions of Black peo-

ple in history. In addition to this there is a full discussion, exercises and activities, which explore representations of Black people in the media and popular literature.

IDEOLOGY

There were negative preconceptions of Black people prior to slavery. The Elizabethans, for example, had certain ideas about Black people being both libidinous as well as lecherous (as illustrated through the work of Hogarth). A precise and sophisticated racist ideology came into being at the same time as modern slavery with the 'discovery' of the New World in 1492. As stated above, slavery would have been impossible without a way of justifying it. Fryer (2) states the following about slavery in his book *'Black People In The British Empire'* :

" Racist ideology sprang from slavery. It arose as a justification of the enslavement of Black people in the New World. At the very heart of the new capitalist system that was clawing its way into world supremacy there was a tragic anomaly. This anomaly had three aspects. The rising capitalist class depended for its very existence on free labour; yet it made extensive use of slave labour as a spring board. It harnessed to production a whole series of technological advances; yet it depended extensively on the most backward and ineffective method of production. It proudly inscribed freedom of the individual on its banner; yet it not only conquered, absorbed, and reinforced servile labour systems throughout the world but also created new ones, including systems of chattel slavery, on an unprecedented social scale and at an unprecedented level of violence. This class therefore required a violent racism not merely as an ideological rational but as a psychological imperative."

Winthrop D. Jordon (3) informs us that initially, before the voyages of John Hawkins in the 1560s,

" *English contact with Africans did not take place primarily in a context which prejudiced the Negro as a slave, at least not as a slave to English men. Rather, Englishmen met Africans merely as another sort of man.*"

Having said this the English already had at their disposal a...

" *concept of blackness (which) was loaded with intense meaning. Long before they found that some men were black, Englishmen found the idea of blackness a way of expressing some of their most ingrained values. No other colour except white conveyed so much emotional impact.*" *Jordon (ibid.)*

Racism gained a firm foothold in the 1600s with the birth of European science, for now it became possible to 'prove' *scientifically* that Black people were different, but not only were they different, they were also inferior. This point was later argued in the work of scientists such as David Hume, John Locke and Edward Long. Hume arguing that Black people were "*naturally inferior to whites..*". Whites having the monopoly on civilization, art, science and talent. After all African society was a non-society for it was not theirs after colonisation:

" *Africans had no artistic culture because there were no cathedral spires in the Kalahari; they were primitive because they were naked and Britons had been naked when they were primitive; they had always been backward because they were backward now; if they advance it would take them centuries because it had taken Europe centuries.*" *(ibid.)*

Such contorted and distorted logic has been the trade mark of racism ever since and goes some way to explain why there is so much mis-information about Black people, and why there still exists so many negative preconceptions, stereotypes and prejudicial 'reasoning' and decision making vis-a-vis them.

When looking at the ideology used to justify colonisation and empire and what Stuart Hall has described as the "*internal*" or "*mainland colonisation*" of Black people in contemporary Britain, we find the development of the most subtle and sophisticated of all racisms - one which, by now has been normalised to such a great extent that it has become "common sense knowledge". A knowledge that very few know the direct origins of, but most believe to be "naturally" and "knowingly" right in the scheme of things. A racism which, in large measure, serves to explain the position of Black people in contemporary British society.

In a concise way Fryer charts the history of the development of racist ideologies from the 1800s onwards:

using **Phrenology**, " *racism told the British that they were ruling over peoples who, unlike themselves, lacked force of character. This pseudo-science deduced people's character from the shape of their skulls.*" ;

using **Teleology**, "*racism told the British that black people had been put on the earth expressly to work for white people, especially in the tropics.*" ;

using **Evolutionism**, " *racism told the British that black people were to be feared, hated, fought and, ultimately, exterminated.*" ;

using **Anthropology**, "*racism told the British that black people were closer to apes than to Europeans; that they were intellectually inferior to Europeans; that they needed to be humanized, civilized and controlled; and that these tasks could be performed only by white people.*" ;

using **Social Darwinism**, " *racism told the British that black people were intellectually inferior to white people and doomed to extinction. This view was propagated by Benjamin Kidd in Social Evolution (1894); by Sir Francis Galton, founder of the 'science' of eugenics; and by Galton's pupil Karl Pearson, for whom exterminated inferior races were stepping-stones for the physically and mentally fitter races.*" ;

and by using **Anglo-Saxonism** racism, " *told the British that God had fitted precisely them to rule over others; that the British constitutional and legal systems were the freest, fairest and most efficient in the world; and the lesser, 'degenerate' races were better off dead.*" *Fryer (ibid).*

IMAGES OF BLACK PEOPLE

As we have seen, slavery was made possible through the conscious use of the sophisticated ideology which was used to justify it. The stereotypical images and negative expectations which inform this ideology are still very much *"alive and kicking"* in popular literature, in songs, in pictures, in television advertisements and on the high street billboard. Alice Walker (4) recognises this when she comments:

> *"I see our brothers and sisters, mothers and fathers, captured and forced into images they did not devise."*

From the introductory notes of *'White On Black - Images of Black People In Western Culture'* the exhibitions' curators note:

> *"The conscious or unconscious acceptance of the stereotyped image of Black people is partly responsible for the persistence of prejudices and racism. The Black sector of the population is daily confronted by the negative consequences of these images which are not of their own making."* (5).

Through a series of quotes we now turn to the examination, in some detail, of the cause and of the effect of racism, and of the ways in which Black people, particularly African people, have been portrayed by the dominant, or mainstream Western culture. We ask you to consider the question, "How influential are these images"?

The unique feature of slavery as practised by white Europeans against Africans has been put like this:

> *"To the Romans, slaves were merely vulgar and conquered people who had no rights of Roman citizenship. The Greeks thought of their slaves as unfortunate peo-*

ple who had failed to cultivate their minds and wills and were thus reduced to that lowly, but necessary state. But these slaves were still human beings. However, the African who was unfortunate enough to find himself on some fast clipper ship to the New World was not even accorded membership of the human race." (6)

How else could such an horrific and brutal institution have existed without such an ideology? The cruelty of the "menstealers" surely shows that mans inhumanity to man knows no bounds. With such a collection of ideas and beliefs, anything becomes possible.

Therefore, as a necessary part of the process which justified slavery, people, both Black and white, had to be brainwashed. Cultural racism became institutionalised and there were no boundaries.

In her book, Dorothy Broderick (7) undertook an historical, literary and critical analysis of the portrait of Black people that emerged from children's books published between 1827 and 1967. In the chapter dealing with slavery she writes:

> *"The need to make slaves less than human had its basis in Christianity, for accepting slaves as human beings with souls, created by the same God the white man worshipped, would be against Christian ethics. Only if slaves were not real people could the good Christian profess that God had intended slavery as part of his scheme of the world."*

Indeed, even the concept of God, the prophets and disciples, angels and so forth, have been given racial characteristics in Judeo-Christian traditions. The image of God being like a particular people can give them an unholy perspective on themselves and others. But so strong are such images that many British born people, both Black and white, many Caribbean people and many African people close their eyes and see a particular God who is traditionally poised, and traditionally coloured.

In the 19th century, the brilliant African Christian theologian, social historian and Cambridge graduate, Edwin Blyden wrote:

"No one can deny the great aesthetic and moral advantages which have accrued to the Caucasian race from Christian art, through all of its stages of development, from the Good Shepherd to the Catacombs, to the transfiguration of Raphael, from rough mosaics to the irrepressible delicacy and beauty of Giotto and Fra Angelico. But to the Negro, all of these exquisite representations exhibited only the physical characteristics of a foreign race; and while they tended to quicken the taste and refine the sensibilities of that (Caucasian) race, they had only a depressing influence upon the Negro who felt that he had neither part nor lot so far as his physical character was concerned in these splendid representations... To him the painting and sculpture of Europe as instruments of education had been worse than failures. They had raised barriers in the way of his normal development." (8).

Colour prejudice, as we have seen, was enhanced and coded into language during the 15th - 17th centuries, as dictionaries and encyclopaedias gave 'white' and 'black' increased significance and value. If you look up the word Black as a descriptive word, in any dictionary or thesaurus, you will find negative definitions, synonyms and symbolism such as: evil; wicked; sullen; nasty; unlucky; gruesome etc. The opposite is the case for white which is associated with purity, goodness, honesty etc. White is seen as the positive part of a universal dichotomy.

The Reverend Martin Luther King, one of the leaders of the Black American Civil Rights and Human Rights Movement in the 1960s, was sensitive to the damaging effects and definitions which create distortions in both Black and white minds and called for a review and change in the use of the English language.

We have seen how images and language establish ideas and the intentions of the ruling white powers were to justify slavery and establish the inferiority of Black people. This point is illustrated in an article written by Nayaba Aghedo (9) in the arts magazine *'Artrage'*. In her review of Anandi Ramamurthy's exhibition *'Black Markets'* she writes:

"So what is the basic context for this intense centuries - old perversion of the cultures and realities of other peoples? Britain and the rest of Europe needed to uphold ideas of superiority. It was the only justification for the enslavement and subjugation of other people of the globe. A people which considered itself civilized had to create a digestible context for its savagery against others."

'Black Markets' is an exhibition of the representation of Black people in advertising. Anandi Ramamurthy, the exhibition's originator, wanted to produce an exhibition which would take a critical look at racist imagery. She writes:

"If they could sell our bodies and rape the wealth of our land, I wondered how they would use our image in the selling of everything from products and services to companies and ideologies. My intention was not to suggest that the context of every image used was racist but rather to understand the exploitative nature of these images in the light of British history." (10)

In relation to the presentation of Black people on television, particularly through advertising, we have to critically examine the roles that they are expected to step into. It is impossible to divorce them from the historical relationship between Black and white people. Consider the adverts that feature Black people on television, billboards and in magazines. How do they reinforce popular stereotypes and myths about Black people? Listed below are a few of the more popular ones:

(1) Frank Bruno in his cameo role of Man Friday (sauce advertisement);
(2) Poor little Colin in "remote" Africa thanks British Petroleum for his education;
(3) Murphy's Irish Stout - "Whether you're Irish or not";
(4) Benneton's - Black man and white man chained together; white dog kisses Black sheep; Black woman breast-feeding white baby.
(5) Robinson's jam - Golliwog logo;
(6) Um Bongo/Kia Ora;
(7) Vitalite.

(8) *Drifter chocolate bar with stereotypical 'pimp' character.*

There are many examples, some of which will be explored in greater detail in Part Two.

The visual image illicits and perpetuates stereotypes, ideas of inferiority, dependency, nationalism, sexuality, thoughts of wet-nursing, slavery times and so on.

When campaigns against Robinson's Golliwog image required a response from the company's marketing manager we are informed in 'Artrage' that he proclaimed:

> *"The Golly is part of our national tradition, an attack on it is an attack on part of Britain's culture." (ibid)*

Comics, magazines and visual images are readily, and regularly, accessible to young people, and as such form a central part in the socializing process. They are important in informing and perpetuating our social and historical consciousness.

> *"To the extent that racism in books conditions children of the dominant group so that they cannot relate to people of other 'races', their human potential is stunted." (11).*

Educationalist and author, Rae Alexander believes that material should be excluded if it contains even one negative stereotype, if it fails to provide strong characters as role models or if it is inappropriate for an all Black, all white or integrated classroom. She writes:

> *"Underlying these criteria was my own experience with many teachers who are insensitive to the racist content of books or who are not equipped to handle such material adequately in their classes. The tragedy is that so many teachers fail to expose racist material for what it is and they fail to make use of it as a basis for discussing prejudice." (12).*

Also in 1975 David Milner (13) made the following conclusions based on surveys of comics:

> *" They encouraged outdated and dangerously hostile views of 'foreign' nations and Black people are largely omitted from comics and derogated in their few appearances. While comics are fantasy materials, we have seen that they have real consequences. Their treatment of Black people can only foster ignorance and divisiveness in a multiracial society."*

A study of British comics in 1985 showed that things were much the same and is described in detail in Part Two. Further studies in Britain in the 1990's confirm that little has changed.

LEARNING OUTCOMES

a) Pupils and students will be aware of how slavery was justified, what is meant by the term ideology and how ideologies 'work'. This will enable them to understand how Europeans were able to participate in slavery.

b) Pupils and students will gain an insight into how Africa and Africans were viewed prior to slavery, how and why this view changed and realise that there were already negative conceptions about Blackness within popular British culture prior to contact with Africa - this meant that Elizabethans, for example, were able to formulate opinions of Black people before ever meeting any.

c) Pupils and students will be able to grasp the fact that there is a direct link between the contemporary experiences of Black people and the experiences of Black people, from the 1600s onwards. They will be aware that this commonality of experience relates directly to racism and the ideologies which perpetuate it.

d) Pupils and students, through a series of exercises, will be in a position to challenge their own presuppositions of Black people and understand concepts such as propaganda, racism, ideologies, stereotypes, prejudice and discrimination.

NATIONAL CURRICULUM

A) Through a reading of primary and secondary source information pupils and students will be able to draw their own conclusions from the evidence presented to them.

B) Pupils and students will be able to critically evaluate theories and ideas which seek to explain differences between individuals.

C) Pupils and students will be aware that there is more than one interpretation of an historical fact and that there are specific vested interests involved when presenting the 'facts' on any incident. The facts used to justify the treatment of Africans during slavery being a case in point.

D) Through a development of a true understanding of the institution of slavery pupils will be able to gain a sense of understanding of how Africans experienced it and how the remnants of slavery still bear upon the lives of people today.

REFERENCES

(1) **Hans Koning** - *'Columbus And His Enterprise'*. Latin American Bureau 1976.

(2) **Peter Fryer** *'Black People In The British Empire - An Introduction'*. Pluto Press 1984.

(3) **Winthrop D. Jordon.** *'The Backness Without'*. Reproduced in *'The Whiteman's Burden'* Oxford University Press 1974

(4) **Alice Walker** - *'Ethnic Notions, Images of Blacks in White Minds'*. Published in 1982.

(5) Exhibition: *'White On Black - Images Of Black People In Western Popular Culture'*. 1990.

(6) **Imamu Amira Baraka** *'Blues People: Negro Music In White America'*. New York 1963.

(7) **Dorothy Broderick** *'Images Of The Black In Children's Fiction'*. London 1973.

(8) **Edward Blyden** *'Christianity, Islam and The Negro Race'*. Pub by W.B. Wittingham 1888.

(9) **Nayaba Aghedo** Comment on 'Black Markets'. Artrage Summer 1991

(10) **Anandi Ramamurthy** *'Black Markets'* Exhibition 1991.

(11) **World Council Of Churches** *'Racism In Children's And School Textbooks'*. Published in 1978.

(12) **Rae Alexander** *'Racist And Sexist Images In Children's Books'*. Published in 1975.

(13) **David Milner** *Survey of Comics.* Research in 1975.

Negative Images of Black people in product advertising and service provision.

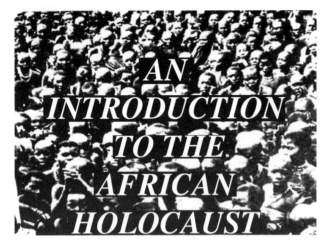
AN INTRODUCTION TO THE AFRICAN HOLOCAUST

Conclusion

The main aim of *'An Introduction To The African Holocaust'* has been to give Black people a true sense of the role that their forebearers played, and how much they have paid, before, during and since their major dispersal from Africa during the period of modern slavery. In addition to this we have tried to present a balanced view of that historical period. Through a Black perspective we have attempted to show the role that Black people had in liberating themselves from slavery. We have, we believe, achieved this through looking at how Black people made slavery unworkable, how they rebelled against slavery through uprisings and how they campaigned against slavery.

Further to this we hope that all students and teachers, through a reading of Parts One and Two, are able to appreciate more fully the true history of the African diaspora and their experience of slavery.

Throughout the book the Black History Resource Working Group has been mindful of the need to expose the 'facts' about slavery and to show the real relationship between Liverpool and the slave trade. A relationship which has, we feel, been shrouded in mystery and half truths. The full history of this relationship is yet to be properly documented - this we acknowledge, hence the use of the word *"Introduction"* in our title.

A recent inquiry into race relations in Liverpool (1989) called *'Loosen The Shackles'*(1) made a number of important points regarding history and the way in which Liverpool institutions, particularly museums, and 'complete' histories, have denied Black people access to their own history on the one hand, whilst at the same time distorting the partial histories which have been presented. The inquiry team explain:

" ..there is a scarcely known people's history, one of the resistance and achievements of Black people in the face of huge diversity, which deserves to be further researched and published."

"We recommend that Liverpool museums and public institutions, when they present Liverpool's history, give a full and honest account of the involvement of Black people in the city."

"Modern Liverpool, while being aware of its shameful history, appears to try hard to gloss over it, if not forget it."

With reference to the last quote, a glaring illustration of attempts to *"gloss over"* the past relates to the Liverpool Town Hall and a number of images which appear about 25 feet up from street level above one of its many windows on the Exchange Street East side.

Below are quotes which refer to the Town Hall; also a photograph which is taken of the Town Hall and is a duplication of the image on the cover of *'An Introduction'*. Also bear in mind the important skills which we have endeavoured to develop in pupils and students through Part Two; the joint skills of drawing conclusions from evidence, and being able to spot when vested interests are at work.

From, *'Know Your Liverpool - Walks In The City'*(2) published in 1974 and reprinted and revised in 1976 and 1979, the following quote describes the carvings on the frieze of the Town Hall:

" Although the allegorical carvings in the frieze relate to the commerce of Liverpool and include a number of human heads they do not, as some of the city's detractors would have it, include heads of negro slaves."

From, *'The Liverpool Privateers - With An Account Of The Liverpool Slave Trade'*(3):

" The insignia of the men-stealers were boldly exhibited for sale in the shops and warehouses, and advertised in the papers. Busts of blackamoors and elephants, emblematical of the African trade, adorned the Exchange or Town Hall."

" Between the capitals runs an entablature or fillet, on which are placed in base relief the busts of blackamoors and elephants, with the teeth of the latter with such emblematical figures representing the African trade and commerce" 'History Of Liverpool'. (author unknown)

The fact that right up until 1979, and in some circles up to the present day, the connection between Liverpool and slavery has been denied seems quite incredible in the face of the overwhelming evidence which puts it so firmly in the centre of the slave trade.

"...still the popular perception of the growth of 18th century Liverpool is that it was very largely funded by the slave trade. Documentary evidence for this view appears to be limited to the celebrated utterance of a drunken actor to the effect that every brick of the detestable town was cemented by the blood of negroes. " (4)

Some may think it hardly surprising that such views are given considering the ignoble nature of such an historical legacy. But denying a history does not make it go away. Facing up to the past and exploring its implications will lead to a greater assurance that, through the process of remembering, such a dehumanising and humiliating thing as chattel slavery can never happen again.

**Black History Resource Working Group
March 1995 - Revised June 1997**

REFERENCES

(1) **The Gifford Inquiry: Gifford, Brown & Bundy** *'Loosen The Shackles'*. Karia Press 1989.

(2) **Thomas Lloyd-Jones** - *'Know Your Liverpool - Walks In The City'*. Workers' Educational Association 1974.

(3) **G.Williams** *'The Liverpool Privateers -With An Account Of Liverpool'*. William Heinemann 1891.

(4) **Adrien Jarvis** *'Liverpool Central Docks 1799-1905, An Illustrated History'*. Published by the National Museums and Galleries on Merseyside and Alan Sutton 1991.

Below, detail from frieze of Liverpool Town Hall. Above, African head from entrance to house on Ullett Rd, Liverpool

58

PART TWO

EXERCISES, ACTIVITIES AND LEARNING MATERIALS

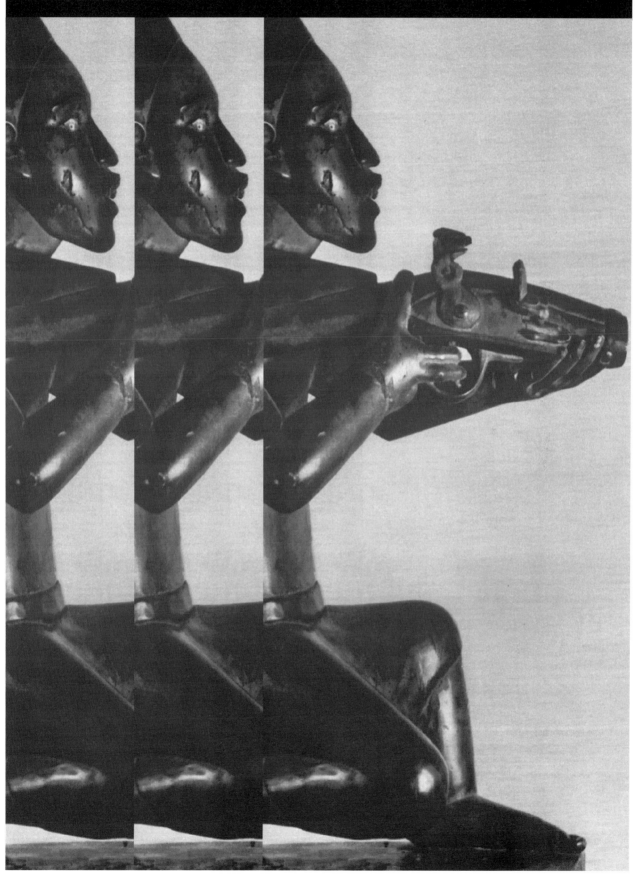

SLAVERY:
An Introduction To The African Holocaust
Revised edition June 1997

CONTENTS (Part Two)

Background image: Detail from Ansdell's
'Hunted Slaves'. Walker Art Gallery

Bronze head found at Wunmonije, Ife, in 1938-39. The head may be a portrait of Oni, Chief of the Ife.

*T*he main aim of this section is to inform pupils and students that slavery is an historical institution that has existed for about 10,000 years. It is also important that pupils and students realise that there were different types of slavery, but that modern slavery, or chattel slavery, differed significantly from anything that preceded it.

Teachers should take the opportunity to reproduce some of the information presented in Part One and present this to pupils and students in a condensed form. The following questions should be asked:

a) What are the two main types of slaves?
b) What evidence is there that slavery existed in ancient India?
c) What evidence is there that there were slaves in Ancient Egypt and in Rome?
Find out more information about the role that slaves played in Egyptian society, paying particular attention to:

* *what tasks they performed;*
* *whether they had any rights;*
* *how they were captured;*
* *how they helped to build the great pyramids;*
* *how they were treated.*

d) Pupils and students should be encouraged to find out who the first slaves were and where the word "slave" originated from. There were slaves in ancient African societies, but the Africans did not call those who they captured during war "slaves". Find out more about slavery in West African societies.

e) There was slavery in Britain. The Romans when they occupied the country enslaved local people. Find out more about life in Britain under Roman occupation. How did this form of slavery differ from modern slavery? Continental Europe, France, Spain, Italy, Germany, Portugal and Britain all had slavery. In England about 10% of the population entered into the Domesday Book in 1086 were slaves. Find out:

* *what type of slaves they were;*
* *what rights they had;*
* *whether they could win, or buy their freedom;*
* *whether they could marry or have any political rights, or rights to property.*

f) Find out why the 'discovery' of the New World by Christopher Columbus in 1492 and his envoy is central to the understanding of modern slavery. Pupils should be able to answer the following questions:

* *why did Columbus enslave the people of the New World?*
* *why did the vast majority of the population of the New World die off?*

Hans Koning states,
"...an estimated one half of the entire population of Hispaniola was killed, or killed themselves, during the first two years of the brothers Columbus' administration. The estimates run from 125,000 to half a million .... In 1515 there were not more than 10,000 Indians left alive; twenty five years later the entire nation had vanished from the earth".(1)

* *Find out Why Bartoleme de las Casas asked the permission of Queen Isabella and King Ferdinand of Spain to import Africans as slaves to work in Hispaniola and other parts of the New World.*

MAPS AND OTHER VISUAL MATERIALS

a) Pupils and students should be given the opportunity to study a number of visual images which show a variety of forms of slavery in different countries and at different points in time. Pupils should be asked specific questions in order to support information already given to them. They should be asked to state:

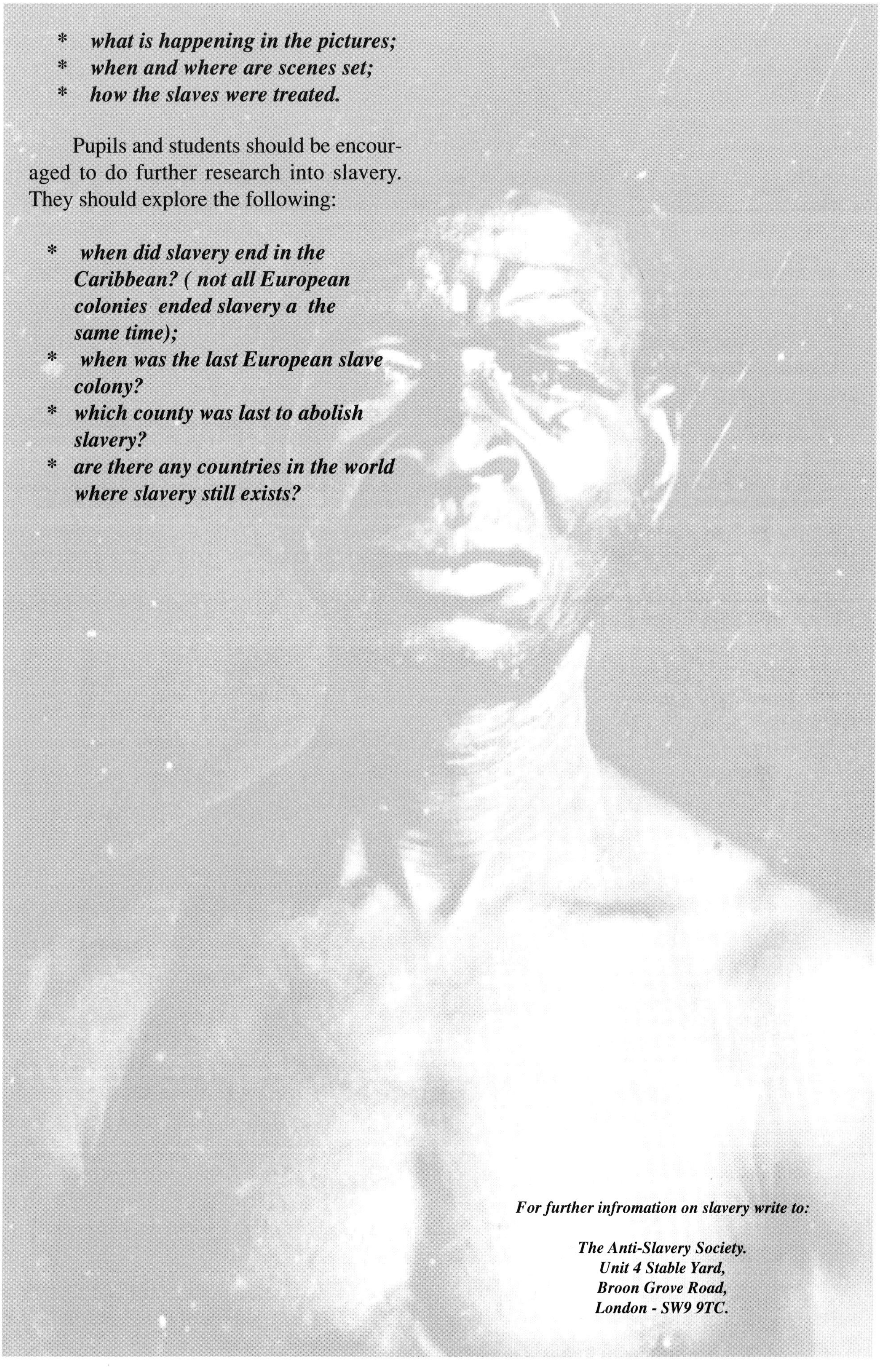

* *what is happening in the pictures;*
* *when and where are scenes set;*
* *how the slaves were treated.*

Pupils and students should be encouraged to do further research into slavery. They should explore the following:

* *when did slavery end in the Caribbean? (not all European colonies ended slavery a the same time);*
* *when was the last European slave colony?*
* *which county was last to abolish slavery?*
* *are there any countries in the world where slavery still exists?*

For further infromation on slavery write to:

The Anti-Slavery Society.
Unit 4 Stable Yard,
Broon Grove Road,
London - SW9 9TC.

64

Fig 1. (top) On the left of this stone engraving from the Kushite religious centre at Musawarat as-Safia, near Meroe, a war elephant follows a file of prisoners-of-war, two of whom can been seen on the right. The engraving was made about 230BC

Fig 2. (bottom) A reconstruction of a Roman slave market: a boy, a young man and five girls await sale with their histories and prices on labels around their necks. Records of slave sales in Rome date from around the 5th century BC.

Fig 3. (top)   Slave boys from Britain on sale in a Roman market - around 6th century BC.

Fig 4. (bottom) A slave market in Lagos: A thriving trade in human beings was set up in the mid 1400s when Prince Henry's explorers rounded Cape Bojodor. Expeditions from 1441 onwards brought back captives, from whom Prince Henry (of Portugal) tried to find out about their country, and whom he tried to convert to Christianity. Others however, saw the captives as the basis of a lucrative trade, the slave trade.

Fig 5. (left) A Dutch slave auction in New Amsterdam, the future New York, early 1660s.

Fig 6. *'Jack'*, (Bottom left) a slave from the Guinea coast who served as a slave driver for a Mr B.F.Taylor. This photograph was taken in Columbia, South Carolina in 1850. It is one of three and is believed to be one of the earliest photographs of a slave in which the subject is identified. *'Jack'* was born in Africa.

Back ground image: Babylonian slaves build a fort under the lash of the overseer. In about 1800 BC slaves in Babylon were divided into two grades: native and foreign. Foreign slaves were prisoners of war and natives slaves often lost their freedom through indebtedness or crime.

AFRICA AND THE CARIBBEAN PRIOR TO SLAVERY

*T*he main aim of this section is to show that prior to the arrival of Europeans in Africa and the Caribbean that there already existed structured societies. Also, with reference to African societies in particular, such societies were sophisticated. They had their own culture and art forms and their own political and social systems.

ANCIENT EGYPT

What evidence is there from the pictures and the text that there were civilized societies in the Nile valley of Egypt? Find out about ancient Egyptian societies and their achievements in terms of:

* *agriculture;*
* *science and mathematics;*
* *medicine;*
* *the visual arts, particularly sculpture and paintings;*
* *music, dance and drama;*
* *astronomy;*
* *building and architecture;*
* *religion;*
* *politics and culture.*

SAHARA CIVILIZATIONS

Figures 5 and 6 are photographs taken from rock paintings in caves in the Sahara desert. These paintings are about 3,000 years old. Examine them closely and answer the following questions:

* *What is happening in figure 5?*
* *How can you tell that Sahara civilizations had domesticated animals?*
* *Describe what you think is happening in figure 6. Are the images of people? What are the figures in the drawing doing?*

* *Find out what was happening in Britain 3,000 years ago. In your research focus on the following: what people ate; how they prepared their food; what kind of weapons they used and what clothes they wore.*
* *From the pictures list all the reasons why you think African civilizations were advanced.*

KUSH- MEROITIC CIVILIZATIONS

Kush is the name which was given by the ancient Egyptians to the kingdoms which lay south of their borders. The kingdom became important in the time of the Meroitic people, and was the most ancient of the independent kingdoms of Africa. The Kushites erected many grand buildings. Tombs have been excavated which have shown many fine jewels, glassware and bronze. Examine figures 1 and 2 and answer the following questions:

a) Why do you think that writing would be important to the development of a civilization? Find out more about hieroglyphics. When were they first translated into European languages and by whom?

b) Figure 2 shows Kushite weapons, how do these compare to European weapons of the same period. Why would weapons have been important to the Kushites?

c) Study the figures 3 and 4 and answer the following questions:

* *how would the masks have been made?*
* *what tools do you think the sculpters used?*
* *what art were Europeans producing at this time?*
* *find out more about the influence that African art has had on European art forms.*

THE CARIBBEAN

Teachers should reproduce some of the information given in Part One and encourage pupils and students to carry out further research.

Before the arrival of the Spanish in the Caribbean, Amerindians had lived there for thousands of years. Over a period of about 50,000 years they had probably travelled from Alaska (having crossed the Bering Straits) down through Central America, to the south, then crossed to the various Caribbean islands. Over thousands of years the islands were populated.

Study the information on South American and Caribbean societies and answer the following questions:

The Aztecs and the Incas - what were these societies like? Did they have religions? Were they farmers or hunters? What type of buildings did they live in? Did they have art and culture?

When Christopher Columbus arrived in the Caribbean the main groups of people living there were the *Arawaks and the Caribs*. Find out more details about these two groups of people paying particular attention to the following:

* *the differences between them;*
* *how they lived;*
* *how they gathered their food;*
* *whether they farmed, killed wild animals or foraged for food;*
* *did they have art and culture?*
* *is there any evidence of political or social systems among these peoples?*

Fig 3.

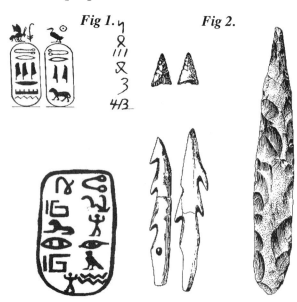

Fig 1.

Fig 2.

Fig 4.

Fig 5.

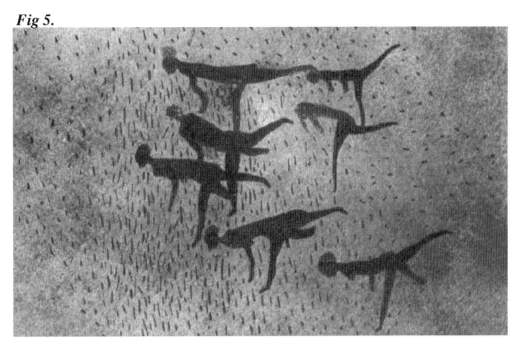

Fig 6.

Fig 7.

Fig 8.

Fig 1. Some of the earliest writing known (dating from about 2000 - 500 BC). Figure 1 features the name Tanyidamani, written in Egyptian hieroglyphs, Meroitic cursive and Meroitic hieroglyphs.

Fig 2. Stone Age craftsmanship from East Africa: hollow arrowheads; bone fishing harpoon and spearhead and lance head from Kenya.

Fig 3. Ivory carving from Benin.

Fig 4. Egyptian gold mask - 22nd Dynasty.

Fig 5. Sahara cave drawing. Graceful Women gathering wild grain.

Fig 6. Sahara cave drawing. Drawing water about 1000 BC; two men work drawing water with a leather bucket. An ox can be seen drinking from a trough.

Fig 7. African Bow lyre. Leather, wood and string - 1700s.

Fig 8. Early Caribbean comb. Wood with bird motif - Aucaner

Fig 9. Caribbean table with snake motif.

Fig 10. Carib Indian - Caribbean

Fig 11. African drum. Akim Accra Ghana.

Fig 9.

Fig 10.

Fig 11.

AFRICA - MANKIND'S BIRTH PLACE

Africa has been described as the *"cradle of mankind"* - there is little doubt that it is the place where early man evolved; it is the place where Stone Age man first drew scenes on the walls of caves giving us an insight into the daily activities of a people who lived thousands of years ago. Early Africa was the place where fire was first used, where simple weapons were developed and where the first early technology was used. It has been described as a place of great architecture, culture and civilization. Africa is the place where the pyramids were built and where man first practised medicine. Africa is the birth place of the sciences.

Early mathematical equations enabled the Egyptians to calculate how to build the pyramids. An in-depth knowledge of star constellations enabled early African man to navigate, not only by land, but across the worlds great oceans.

It was a sophisticated Africa continent that the Portuguese and Spanish 'discovered'. One that had already:

- *seen the evolution of Homo Sapiens around about 100,000 BC;*
- *Africans in the Sahara raising cattle - around 5000 BC;*
- *the development of early Egyptian civilization - about 3000 BC;*
- *seen the rise of Axum in Northern Ethiopia - 100 BC;*
- *many powerful kingdoms such as those of Pharaohs, Kushites, Nubians and Saracens.*

THE SEA OF DARKNESS

In the early 1400s, no Portuguese mariner had sailed any further south than the Canary Islands, 800 miles southwest of Portugal. South of the Canary Islands was the *"Sea Of Darkness"* and, what came to be known as Cape Bojador (1). So fearful of travelling southwards were the Portuguese that few dared risk the journey for the sake of mere exploration. They believed that:

" beyond this cape there is no population, no water, neither trees nor green herbs; and the sea is so shallow that a league from the shore its depth is hardly a fathom. The tides are so strong that any ship which passes the cape will never be able to return." (ibid).

After several attempts, on the instructions of Prince Henry, to pass southwards beyond the Canary Islands, Gil Eannes eventually reached Cape Bojador in 1434. In fact he had passed beyond it and bought back some plants - St. Mary's roses - to show the Prince what grew there.

Although in terms of distance Eannes had not covered a great area, around 150 miles south of the Canary Islands, he had crossed the barrier of fear, and conquered the *"Sea of Darkness"*.

Successive voyages were made to the Cape and journeys were made inland on horseback. The Portuguese made contact with Africans with whom their mission was to, *"speak with these people or capture some of them" (ibid)* and establish whether they were Moors or Gentiles. On an expedition in 1436 under Baldaya, the Portuguese failed in this mission, in fact they were confronted by 19 men armed with spears and were lucky to escape with their lives. In order to avoid going back to Portugal empty-handed Baldaya, having noticed the abundance of seals in the bay, killed as many as he could and returned home with their skins.

Expeditions from 1441 onwards bought back captives, from whom Prince Henry tried to find out about their country. He also tried, with modest success, to convert them to Christianity. The Portuguese soon saw that there was a lucrative trade to be exploited, that of the trade in humans, the slave trade.

THE CARIBBEAN

In 1492 Christopher Columbus sailed west in the service of Spain in search of the Indies. He 'discovered' San Salvador, Cuba and Hispaniola, although, until the end of his life he believed that he had reached the Orient.

What Columbus had 'discovered' was about 200,000 people who had been living in the Caribbean Islands for about 1000 years. The history of the indigenous people of America goes back further, it begins in prehistoric times. It is thought that hunters first entered America over 50,000 years ago following animals across the land or ice bridge which then joined Alaska to Asia. Before the bridge disappeared many other groups of hunters followed, pushing those who had come before them further south. 5,000 years later their descendants were the Mayas, Incas and the Aztecs who were met by the Spanish and Portuguese during their voyages of 'exploration'.

Fig 1.

Columbus quickly colonised several of the islands in the Caribbean and set the inhabitants to work. Their task was to search for gold which Columbus believed to exist in huge quantities. He believed the Caribbean to be an El Dorado where gold nuggets could be found which were as large as goose eggs (indeed this is what he reported Queen Isabella and King Ferdinand on his return to Spain). The native Amerindians were worked to death in their elusive search; only able to find minuscule quantities of gold, they were subject to many atrocities. They had limbs chopped off, they were burned and disembowelled.

Fig 2.

When it became clear that there was little to be gained through the search for gold, and after a significant proportion of the natives had either been murdered or had died due to contracting European diseases for which they had no immunity, the attention of the Spanish was drawn to sugar

Fig 3.

After most of the inhabitants had died, Batholome de las Casas, a priest, pleaded with Queen Isabella to spare the remaining few Amerindians left, and asked for permission to import Africans to do the work instead. This started the modern period of slavery and the transportation of Africans to the Caribbean.

Fig 1. *Columbus arrives and names his newly discovered island Hisponiola.*
Fig 2. *Caribbean Indians sift and clean gold dust.*
Fig 3. *Amerindians having their hands chopped off for failing to meet the gold dust quota. (from the book by Bartolome de las Casas entitled 'Spanish Cruelties' published in 1609).*
Fig 4. *An Impression of Christopher Columbus.*
Fig 5. *Bartolome de las Casas.*

REFERENCES
(1) Duncan Castlereagh 'The Great Age Of Exploration'. Published by The Readers Digest Association 1971.

Fig 4.

CHRISTOPHER COLUMBUS

Name: Cristoforo Colombo; country of origin was Italy. He was also know as Christobal Colon (Spanish) and as Christopher Columbus in English.

His life: Columbus was born in Genoa, Italy in 1451 and died in Valladolid in Spain in 1506. Columbus was married to Felipa Perestrello Moniz in 1480. He had one son, Diego who was born in 1482.

Background: Not much known of his early years. Son of a middle class weaver; self-educated, ambitious. First sailed as a merchant's clerk, later as a trader on Portuguese ships visiting England, Ireland and the Azores - as well as the Guinea Coast of Africa where the Portuguese had already set up trading posts.

Skills: Learned mathematics, astronomy and several languages (Latin, Pontuguese and Spanish) on his own. Sailing and navigation training on the job. Persuasive talker.

Beliefs: A fervent Catholic (on conversion from Judaism) and strong monarchist.

Goals: To find a Western sea route to China; to find gold for himself and for the Spanish Crown; and to spread Christian values to the 'dark areas' of the globe.

The Voyages: Columbus made four voyages in total. In return for three ships and enough money for a crew and supplies he demanded 10 per cent of all riches found, an Admiralty over the Western Ocean and the governorship of any newly-found land. That he got to the Caribbean at all was the result of a serious navigation error. He miscalculated the distance from Spain to Cipangu (Japan) at 2,400 nautical miles rather than 10,000.

First Voyage: October 12, 1492 - landed on a tiny island in the Bahamas. Columbus then sailed to Cuba and finally Hispaniola. He returned home with a handful of gold trinkets and six Taino Indians who he presented to Queen Isabella and king Ferdinando.

Subsequent Voyages: September 1493; May, 1498; May, 1502. "Meandered around the Caribbean" and landed at Trinidad, Panama, Jamaica, Venezuela, Dominica and several other smaller islands.

Background image - Queen Isabella of Spain.
Columbus biography details from:
'The New Internationalist' - December 1991.

BLACK PEOPLE IN BRITAIN

Exercises, Learning Materials And Activities

*T*here has been a Black presence in Britain for many centuries. There is evidence of Black people, Africans, in Scotland 1800 years ago, evidence of Black people in Ireland in the 900's and many references to Black people in England during Elizabethan times. The main issues in relation to the Black presence in Britain from about 400 years ago are: How they come to be here? What were their experiences ? Were slaves sold in mainland Britain? And why were they brought to England as servants?

THE WILLIAMSON'S LIVERPOOL ADVERTISER

Pupils and students should read through a number of advertisements which give information on slave sales, auctions and details on runaway slaves. They should be made aware of the fact that there is documented evidence of slave sales which shows clearly that slaves were sold in Britain, and in Liverpool in particular. Pupils and students should be aware of the fact that the methods of sale, or auction, in Britain were not the same as in the Americas or in Africa, nor were they on the same scale. They should be asked to draw out the following information from the advertisements:

a) *What indications are there that slaves were seen as a commodity, no different from any other?*

b) *Why do you think that the sellers gave details about the age and the physical condition of the slaves who were to be sold?*

* *What do you think is mean by the following phrases:*

"lively, humane disposition",
" a very serviceable hand",
" for a Guinea Ship".

* *Why do you think that anyone would be interested in purchasing " a vessel from 150 to 250 tons burthen" ?*

* *What was a Guinea merchant?*

* *What evidence is there from the advertisements that slaves and servants were treated badly?*

SLAVES SOLD BY AUCTION ON THE CUSTOM HOUSE STEPS

Teachers should read the section from Dicky Sam's book *'Liverpool and Slavery'*, or reproduce it and give pupils and students the opportunity to read it. The main aim of reading this chapter is for them to get a feel of what a slave sale might have been like. They should also have been given some background information on slavery from teachers notes in this, and preceeding sections. Pupils and students should then be asked the following questions:

a) *How can we tell from reading the chapter that slaves were treated the same as any other cargo?*

b) *Why would people be interested in buying slaves?*

c) *Dicky Sam says that many people came to see the auction because they were curious. Why do you think this was?*

d) *Why do you think that slaves were branded?*

e) *How is it possible to tell that there were people who supported slavery? Who were they?*

f) *Write a short account, either from the point of view of the slaves being sold, or those who had gone to the auction out of curiosity.*

IMAGES OF BLACK PEOPLE IN THE EIGHTEENTH CENTURY

Black people were very much a feature of 18th century Britain: this is evident from the extent to which they feature in paintings and drawings from this period. As Dabydeen puts it:

"Judging from their widespread presence in English art it can be said that they had become very much a part of white society. They are found in the most unexpected places, participating in the society as if they had always been there."

Pupils and students should study the copies of three paintings: *'Henrietta Of Lorraine'* - Van Dyck; *'Duchess Of Portsmouth'* - Mignard and *'Two Girls And A Negro Servant'* -Wright. After studying these, they should answer the following questions:

a) What role do you think the Black characters play in the paintings?
b) Do you think that the presence of a Black person in a painting would have said anything about the status of the white person(s) present?
c) It has been suggested that the presence of a Black person in 17th and 18th century paintings existed merely to reflect upon the superiority of the white. Read Dabydeen's quote and say what you think.

" ..the black is a mere aesthetic foil. The lady's tallness comes out in relation to his smallness, and his dark skin throws into relief the whiteness of her skin."

In the short lived Liverpool Chronicle, James Parker, auctioneer, advertised for sale by candle, at the Merchants' Coffee House,
"..a fine negro boy, 11 years of age, imported from bonny, by Mr. Thomas Yeats, a Guinea Merchant - Cleveland Square".

Pupils and students should be made aware the Black servant was a status symbol who served a specific, often dramatic, purpose in the paintings commissioned by the rich in the 17th 18th centuries. They should be encouraged to explore paintings of this period further noting that the presence of the Black person served the same purpose as: the pet lapdog; the pet lamb and horse. In fact in those paintings which featured both 'negro servant' and dog, in family scenes for example, it is often the case that the dog is given greater importance than the Black person who, as stated, was seen very much as a pet also; the pet Black. These issues can be looked at further through other subjects, particularly art when exploring images of Black people in 17th and 18th century works of art. The linguistic style of the advertisements for the sale of slaves can also be explored through English.

" wanted immediately a negro boy. He must be of deep black complexion, and a lively, and human disposition, with good features, and not above 15, nor under the age of 12. Apply to the printer". Williamson's Advertiser August 20th 1756.

" For sale immediately, one stout negro young fellow, about 20 years of age, that has been employed for 12 months on board ship, and is a very serviceable hand. And a negro boy, about 12 years old, that has been used since September. Last to wait at a table, and is of a very good disposition, both warranted sound. Apply to Robert Williamson Broker. NB. A vessel from 150 to 200 tons burthen is wanted to be purchased".
Willamson's Advertiser - June 24th 1757

William Hogarth's Marriage a la Mode

From Dicky Sam - 'Liverpool And Slavery'

*I*n 1766, the chief topic of interest on the Liverpool Exchange Flags was the price of slaves, sugars and rum: the former article of merchandise being occasionally sold by auction on the Custom House steps.

Here is a specimen of the auctioneer's bill:

Twelve pipes of raisin wine;
two boxes of bottled cyder;
six sacks of flour;
three negro men;
two negro boys;
one negro girl.

Just picture to yourself, after the auctioneer has disposed of his first lots, he comes to the more important, namely, the selling of the slaves. The crowd has greatly increased, many have heard that blacks were to be sold, and therefore, they have, come to satisfy their curiosity. The auctioneer stands on a chair, one of the slaves is brought out of a shed close by; the crowd now jostle one against the other, in order to get a good look at the man to be sold to anyone who will buy him. The auctioneer commences with:

" Now, gentlemen, here is a fine negro, just imported from old Calabar, age about 28, finely proportioned, healthy, and good looking; he would make a good general servant or cook. What shall I say for him? I can give you a clean title with him; you see he is branded DD on the forehead, so you have no fear of losing him. Come, gentlemen, what shall I say for him?"

A voice in the crowd says " £5", the auctioneer replies, " why, he is worth £50, and only £5 offered. Hold up your head Caesar".

At this juncture, a merchant hints to the auctioneer that a drop of rum might help the bidders; the hint is taken, the rum is handed round, and the bidding re-commences - £7; £8.10; £9.10; £10; and so the price gradually advances to £15; ".. going, gone!" At which sum he is knocked down, and delivered to the buyer.

The next bought out is a negro boy , 14 years old, healthy and strong, just from the coast, and would make a good page boy; he has the same brand as the last, no chance of losing him.

" What shall I say for the start?" An old captain offers £3; this is followed by offers of £5; £6.10; £7.10; £9. " Any advance on £9?" Asks the auctioneer; "if not, I must sell him. £9! No advance! Going, gone!" The hammer falls, the negro boy is handed over to his new master, and it seems as though he did not know whether to laugh or cry. At the end of the sale the crowd breaks up, and slowly retrace their steps.

Slaves For Sale

Also, in the same paper of September 8th, 1766, the following advertisement appeared:—"To be sold at the Exchange Coffee House, Water Street, this day, the 12th Sept. inst., at 1 o'clock precisely, eleven negroes, imported per the Angola," . . . . Broker.

Also, in the Jamaica paper, have appeared some very curious advertisements for runaway slaves, with a description of their brands.

[2] In the Jamaica paper called the *Gazette*, of St. Jago de la Vega, dated October 11th, 1787, we number ninety-seven runaway slaves, advertised, viz.: forty-five branded and twenty-two without brands. Among the former is " William, marked on the right shoulder R A, heart and diamond between, and on the left R A, heart at top." Also, " Batty on both shoulders, H P in one and Guy, marked on the right shoulder D, and on the left I H."—In the same Gazette, dated November 8th, 1787, there are notified twenty-three runaways marked, and forty-four unmarked. Among those marked is " Apollo W S, on his face and breast,"—"Robert R P on each cheek, and Kingston marked YORKE on each shoulder and breast."

A Blackamoor boy of eight or nine years of age: Whoever has such a one to dispose of, may hear of a purchaser at Mrs. Cranwell's, over-against (i.e. opposite) the Chapel in Conduit Street. (London Daily Advertiser - December 1744)

RUN AWAY!

From Captain Stubbs. A yellowish Negro man, about five feet seven inches, very flat nose, and a scar across his forehead, he had when he ran away, a white pea-jacket, a pair of black Worsted stockings, and a black wig. Whoever will bring this said Negro to his above mentioned master, Captain Stubbs, shall receive two guineas reward.

NB. The above mentioned master, Captain Stubbs, desires that no commander, merchants, or other gentlemen will employ the above mentioned Negro; he goes by the name of Stephen Brown, and if he will return to his master, nothing will be done to him. (Public ledger December 1761)

RUN AWAY FROM HIS MASTER

"Run away from his Master , a Negro Boy, under five feet in height, about 16 years old, named CHARLES. He is very ill made, being remarkably bow-legged, hollow back'd and pot bellied. He had on, when he went away, a coarse dark brown Linnen Frock, a Thickset Waistcoat, very dirty Leather Breeches, and on his head an old Velvet Jockey Cap.

Whoever will bring him, or give any Tidings of him, to Mr. Beckford in Pall-Mall, may depend upon being very handsomely rewarded."

To be sold at the Exchange Coffee House in Water Street, this day the 12th September, at one o'clock precisely, Eleven Negroes imported per Angola. (Williamson's Advertiser 1766)

1768. A fine Negro boy offered for sale in Liverpool. Is said to be about 4 ft. 5 in. tall, of a sober, tractable, humane (i.e. willing) disposition. Eleven or twelve years of age, talks English very well, and can dress hair in a tolerable way .
(Williamson's Liverpool Advertiser).

Olaudah Equiano & Ignatious Sancho

Olaudah Equiano wrote his life story and of his experience as a slave. He was kidnapped from West Africa when he was ten or eleven, then experienced the notorious Middle Passage as he was shipped from Africa to the Caribbean. Equiano also travelled to America, Canada, Europe and the Arctic.

Equiano came to England in 1757 and was re-sold into slavery five years later. Eventually he was able to buy his freedom. He settled in England and became an avid anti-slavery complainer who travelled the country telling of his experiences and speaking out against slavery.

Ignatious Sancho (painted by Gainsborough in 1768) was born on a slave ship in the Caribbean. He was orphaned when he was still a baby and bought by an Englishman who took him to London. He was employed as a butler in the house of the duke and duchess of Montague.

Sancho corresponded with members of the literary elite attempting to draw their attention to the plight of slaves .

Francis Barber was brought to Yorkshire from Jamaica . He was set free in his master's will on his death in 1782.

Barber had been Mr. Johnson's servant in about 1752 and was sent to school in Bishops Stortford. He lived in Johnson's house off Fleet Street for many years.

When Johnson died in 1782 he left Barber his property, an income of £70 a year and all of his books.

Barber moved to Lichfield, got married to Elizabeth and ran a school until he died in 1801.

Billy Waters was one of the best known Black street entertainers. He was a busker outside of the Adelphi Theatre in the Strand (London). He lived in the Parish of St. Giles.

At the end of the American War of Independence, the number of Black beggers and street entertainers in London increased significantly with an influx of poor Blacks and freed slaves who had been discharged from the services.

Tom Molineaux was one of the most famous of a number of Black boxers who lived in England in the early 1800s. The following is a short extract, reproduced in *'Black Personalities In The Era Of The Slave Trade'* from Pierce Egan's

CRIB AND THE BLACK

On the 18th of December, of a fight I will sing,
when bold Crib and Molineaux entered the ring,
with hope and expectation our bosoms beating high,
while the rain poured torrents from a dark low'ring sky.

Tom Crib is a British man, he's cast in British mould,
with a heart like a lion, of courage, stout and bold,
a brave black man is Molineaux, from America he came,
and boldly tried to enter with Crib the lists of fame.

The Black stripp'd, and appeared of a giant like strength,
large in bone, large in muscle, and with arms a cruel length,
with his skin as black as ebony - Crib's as white as snow,
they shook hands like good fellows, then to it they did go.

The very first round they had, Crib hit him on the head,
but received one in the mouth, and very freely bled;
the two or three next rounds Crib seem'd to have the best,
but the black man most bravely resolved to stand the test.

Then the Black he did rally, oh! How he play'd away,
and shew'd our British hero some terrible hard play;
like light'ning 'bout Crib's napper the blows came left and right,
while the Black's friends felt certain their man would win the fight.

Then the Black still bore on with a terrible force,
the blows fell on poor Tom Crib like kicks from a horse;
his friends e' en were doubtful, "Crib will lose it" they did cry,
never mind says he to Gulley, "I'll be better bye and bye."

Billy Waters

Francis Barber

Tom Molineaux

(left) Tom Molineaux and Tom Crib fight for the heavyweight championship around 1810.

Duchess Of Portsmouth   - National Portrait Gallery.
Painted in 1682.

Henrietta of Lorraine

" The black exists merely to reflect upon the superiority of the white. In Van Dyck's Henrietta of Lorraine (left). The lady's tallness comes out in relation to his smallness, and his dark skin throw into relief the whiteness of her skin". David Dabydeen.

Above left 'Two girls and a Negro Servant'. Joseph Wright 1769/70, oil on canvas - Watney Collection U.K.

Above right 'Black Boy' William Windus (1822/1907) - Walker Art Gallery. Reproduced with the permission of the trustees of the National Museums and Galleries on Merseyside.

THE TRIANGULAR TRADE

Exercise, Learning Materials And Activities

*T*he main activities in this section relate to developing pupils' and students' understanding of what the *'Triangular Trade'* was, how it worked, who benefited and how the role of African Slaves was central to this. *"The whole system was, frankly, regarded as resting on slavery."* (see Teachers Notes).

Using the definition given in *'overview'*, Peter Fryer's description and additional information given by teachers, pupils and students should describe how the triangular trade worked in their own words. Special attention should be paid to the following:

a) **What goods were sent to Africa and where were these goods manufactured?**

b) **Identify, items for trade which were made in Sheffield.**

c) **Identify British cities, apart from Liverpool, which were involved in the slave trade.**

d) **Include details of how slaves were caught in Africa and the role of local chiefs in this activity.**

e) **Explain what the Middle Passage was and how it formed a part of the Triangular Trade.**

f) **What happened to the slaves on arrival in the Americas?**

g) **List the goods which were bought in the Americas and the various methods of exchange.**

h) **Say how the Triangular Trade was self generating.**

i) **Note details about the time that the whole 'triangular' journey, or process, took.**

j) **Describe in detail the role of : bankers; industrialists; merchant capitalists and slave traders.**

OVERVIEW - THE TRIANGULAR TRADE

The Triangular Trade refers to the voyages made by slave ships from Britain, and other European countries. Britain took part in the Triangular Trade from about 1550, while the Spanish and Portuguese took part earlier, from the end of the 1400s.

Ships sailed from England to the West Coast of Africa. On board these ships were various trade goods such as: weapons, textiles, glass beads, iron bars and manillas. When the ships arrived at the coast of Africa these goods would be exchanged for African captives known as slaves. The ship's captain would barter with various traders so that he could get the most slaves he could for the least amount of trade goods.

The ship would probably have to sail to several different locations before it had bought enough slaves to fill up its hull. This part of the voyage could take up to six months. The ship would then set sail for the Caribbean, or mainland America where slaves would be sold to plantation owners.

Plantation owners paid for the slaves they bought with produce such as tea, coffee, cotton, rum or any such trade goods which were in demand in Britain. The ship would then make the final leg of the journey.

Once back in port in England goods bought in the Caribbean and mainland America would be sold for cash. Banks and financiers would be 'paid off' having contributed towards ship purchase, repair or the cost of British manufactured goods; and the profit left was used to finance the next voyage.

The profit made from the Triangular Trade fuelled the British economy. It provided the stimulus needed for industry, for the manufacture of cotton, steel, and the energy which fed them. Eric Williams says that slavery provided a *"..shot in the arm"* for the Industrial Revolution. With reference to Liverpool, slavery transformed it from:

".. an insignificant seaport, a small port of little consequence... a few streets some distance from the creek- or pool- which served as a harbour" to one of the *"..richest and most prosperous trading centres in the world."(1).*

Pupils should explore further the debate about the extent to which slavery facilitated the industrialisation of Britain. They should be encouraged to research this as a cross-curricular theme, specifically through exploring the use of art as a vehicle for examining issues of race and racism.

The Triangular Trade - Illustrations

a) The main aim of using the illustration of the triangular trade is to further reinforce the geographical relationship between Britain, Africa and the Caribbean and to further detail the nature of the trade between those countries. The illustration should be used to stress the physical distance between the countries, the length of the time it took to embark on the Triangular Trade and the goods which were traded, and at which points.

There are clear cross-curricular implications in relation to this exercise, particularly through Geography and art.

Sugar (spice, gold, ivory) and Slavery

" Each of these new beverages, (tea, coffee and chocolate) that British people began to drink in the 1650s had a rather bitter natural taste. So there was a growing demand for sugar, even among the very poor. The increasing popularity of rum punch also promoted sugar consumption in England, which went up four-fold between 1660 and 1700- and about twenty-fold between 1663 and 1775". (Fryer)

Fig 1.

Fig 2.

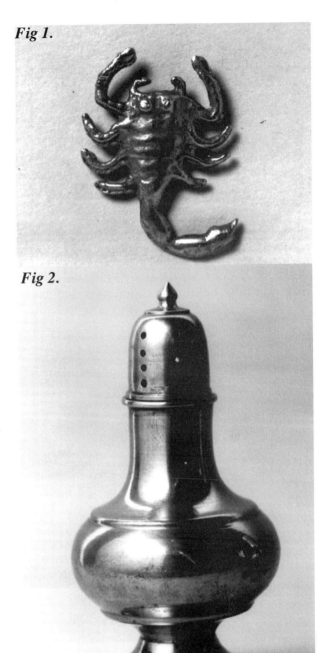

Fig 3.

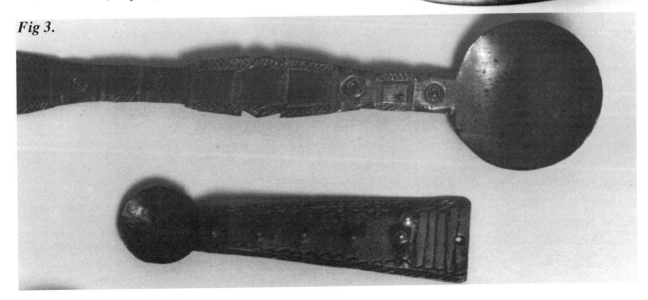

As well as the new demand for sugar there was the demand for ivory, gold and spices. Fig 1. A Gold Scorpion, Central South America. Fig 2. Pepper Pots, pewter 18th century. Fig 3. Two spoons for measuring gold dust, brass, made by the Asante. (All figures from NMGM collection).

"Ships left London, Bristol and Liverpool loaded with textiles made in Lancashire; muskets, brass rods, and cutlery made in Birmingham; copper rods and manillas (bronze rings used as a medium of exchange) made in Glamorgan, Bristol, Warrington, St. Helens, and Flintshire. Cargoes also included gunpowder, felt hats, silk pieces, sailcloth, green glass, beads, spirits, tobacco, and beer brewed by Samuel Whitbread and Sir Benjamin Trueman. On the African coast these commodities were bartered for slaves, who were shipped across the Atlantic on the notorious middle passage. In Barbados and the Leeward Islands, Jamaica and in Suriname these young Africans were exchanged for sugar, spices, molasses, rum and tobacco, which were carried back to England and sold. With a proportion of the profit more manufactured goods were bought, and the cycle began afresh." (Fryer).

THE KORABRA SERIES Pupils and students should be given the opportunity to study the two paintings below and to interpret and ask questions about their meaning.

Two paintings from the seven large works in the series entitled, **Korabra,** meaning *"to go and come back"* in Aken, Ghana, by Gavin Jantjes, in which he attempts to communicate the emotional impact of the scale of the disaster, inhumanity and bitter facts of slavery. In 1983 he re-thought his approach to image making from realism to a more symbolic style to convey some of the brutal meaning in the arts, poems and texts which he researched. The cycle of works moves from Africa, to the sea, to the market-place, to work in the fields, to the city, to a vision of re-birth and defiance. The second painting in the series, with it three coffin-ships, one for each century In which slave ships crossed the Atlantic, treats his response to mass murder, dispossession of Africans from their home lands and the roots of their culture. Yet the enslaved Africans carried their culture with them. The third shows a male and female figure in a suggested market-place against a sweeping sky. Their skin is patched and pale and their necks and sense of identity are as if broken. Black Shadow like figures of women and children stand behind them, looking towards Africa and the crucifix-masts of the ships which have brought them. In their shame and excile, the couple appear like Adam and Eve expelled from paradise.

From the Korabra catalogue, (Caroline Collier 1988) From the Korabra Series, Sand, tissue paper, pigment and acrylic on canvas (1986 and 1985). The two paintings shown are owned by Coventry City Museum & Art Gallery and Wolverhampton Art Gallery, respectively.

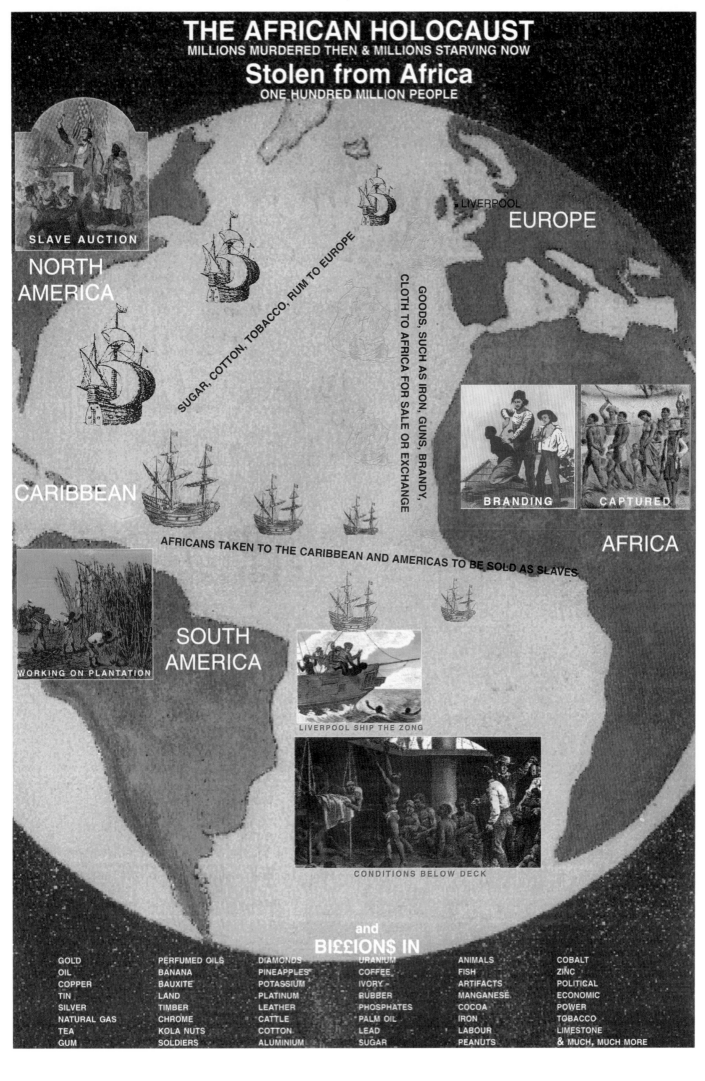

THE AFRICAN HOLOCAUST
MILLIONS MURDERED THEN & MILLIONS STARVING NOW
Stolen from Africa
ONE HUNDRED MILLION PEOPLE

SLAVE AUCTION

NORTH AMERICA

LIVERPOOL

EUROPE

SUGAR, COTTON, TOBACCO, RUM TO EUROPE

GOODS, SUCH AS IRON, GUNS, BRANDY, CLOTH TO AFRICA FOR SALE OR EXCHANGE

BRANDING

CAPTURED

CARIBBEAN

AFRICANS TAKEN TO THE CARIBBEAN AND AMERICAS TO BE SOLD AS SLAVES

AFRICA

WORKING ON PLANTATION

SOUTH AMERICA

LIVERPOOL SHIP THE ZONG

CONDITIONS BELOW DECK

and
BI££ION$ IN

GOLD	PERFUMED OILS	DIAMONDS	URANIUM	ANIMALS	COBALT
OIL	BANANA	PINEAPPLES	COFFEE	FISH	ZINC
COPPER	BAUXITE	POTASSIUM	IVORY	ARTIFACTS	POLITICAL
TIN	LAND	PLATINUM	RUBBER	MANGANESE	ECONOMIC
SILVER	TIMBER	LEATHER	PHOSPHATES	COCOA	POWER
NATURAL GAS	CHROME	CATTLE	PALM OIL	IRON	TOBACCO
TEA	KOLA NUTS	COTTON	LEAD	LABOUR	LIMESTONE
GUM	SOLDIERS	ALUMINIUM	SUGAR	PEANUTS	& MUCH, MUCH MORE

THE LONG MARCH

The march to the coast was an agonising one, with many casualties. Weak slaves would be abondoned by their captors and would await their death. Sometimes slaves were made to travel hundreds of miles to the coast where they would be branded and put into the ship's hold.

Such journeys would be made under the full blaze of the African sun. Slaves would be shackled together either by the hands, or feet or often both. Often they were made to march in pairs, secured together by a length of wood, forked at both ends in order to encpsulate the neck. Biard's painting shows slaves being brought to the coast secured together in horizontal columns, or rows. Escape was rare, overseers were ever present armed with knives and guns and ready to use the whip.

Olaudah Equiano describes the journey that he made to the coast after being kidnapped as one of great fear; fear of the unknown and fear of the white men having observed, first hand, their treatment of Africans.

Slavers scoured the coasts of Guinea for slaves. As each area was "cleared" they would move inland, southwards and westwards. Past the Niger, down the Congo coast, past Angola, round the Cape of Good Hope and even as far as Mozambique on the eastern side of Africa. C.L.R. James in his book 'The Black Jacobins' describes the slave march:

" The slaves were collected in the interior, fastened one to another in columns, loaded with heavy stones of 40 or 50 pounds in weight to prevent attemts to escape, and then marched the long journey to the sea, sometimes hundreds of miles, the weakly and sick dropped to die in the African jungle. Some were brought to the coast by canoe, lying in the bottom of boats for days on end, their hands bound, their faces exposed to the tropical sun and the tropical rain, their backs in the water which was never bailed out ."

Above, and left (detail) Francois Biard's *'The Slave Trade*. Royal Academy, 1840. Used with permission of Hull City Museums And Art Galleries, Wilberforce House.

In 1840 Biard sent his painting to be exhibited at the Royal Academy in London. The scene is set on the West Coast of Africa and illustrates the cruelty and callousness of a number of different types of slave traders. The painting details the suffering and indignity with which African slaves were treated. The picture has been described as, *".an inventory of miseries.. (Honour ibid)*

A writer in The Anthenaeum, a distinguished journal noted for art criticism, in May 1840 remarked on Biard's paining in this way:

" *Few English painters have chosen such a subject ... We are still, happily, in Art, far from that state which, in the search after strong effects, permits the seeker to riot among all that is physically and morally monstrous, hideous, and distorted. We are, however, constrained to add, that few English painters could have treated any subject with so much vigour. It is remarkable, indeed, how the worst moral features of the traffic in human blood have been combined and illustrated, so as to make up the tale. On the one hand, helpless animal suffering is displayed in the wretched groups driven to market, with little more intelligence in their misery than the flock of sheep driven to the shambles - half way, as it were, between the Negro of the creek and the white man of the vessel, - the wretched and brutalized chief, feathered and tricked out in finery, bartering his war captives, or, perhaps, even his own kindred, for luxury and gold, the enjoyments and uses of which only touch his dull senses faintly, - the interpreter counting on his fingers the price of the drove, - the sportsman who has run it down, - the herdsman who has brought it up to the coast for shipment, - and lastly, on the other side, more ghastly still, the supercargo lying listless along, with the ledger, containing such a fearful record of human agony, at his side, and his white ministers binding and branding their pray, with a remorseless indifference as to the deep though ill-expressed feelings of manhood which tyranny and torture are crushing and searing out of the victims for ever."* Reproduced in *'The Image of The Black in Western Art'.* (2)

It is said that Biard made the slave trade, by a single picture, more infamous than it had been depicted by a score of eloquent speeches given by abolitionists and antislavery campaigners. What do **you** make of the painting?

REFERENCES
(1) Ramsey Muir 'A History of Liverpool'. Pub by Williams & Norgate 1907.
(2) Hugh Honour 'The Image of The Black in Western Art'. Pub byHarvard University Press 1989
Background image: Cowrie Shells

THE MIDDLE PASSAGE

Exercises, Learning Materials And Activities

*T*he main activities in this section relate to developing young people's ability to draw out information from written and visual accounts of slavery and the slave trade. Pupils and students should be given time to read through four accounts of the Middle Passage and then they should be asked a number of questions. Teachers can read through the text pointing out the differences in the accounts, focusing on:

  a) *the vested interests that the writer may be bringing to bear to his/her account;*
  b) *the fact that the account written by Equiano was based on his actual experience of the Middle Passage.*

The illustrations of the *'Brookes'* should be used to reinforce the horror of the slave trade and the Middle Passage in particular. Pupils and students should be reminded that the illustration is a true reflection of how Africans made the journey from the African coast to the Caribbean.

(1) **Dicky Sam** - *The Ship Thomas'* (on her journey from Africa to Jamaica).
a) Why would the slaves on board the Thomas have preferred to jump overboard than make their journey into the unknown?
b) How does the writer feel about slavery?
Use points from the text to illustrate your answer.
c) In your own words describe how the Triangular Trade worked.
d) Describe the treatment of the slaves on board ship.
e) Explain the role of the bankers and business men in the slave trade.

(2) **C.L.R. James** - *'The Property'* from *'The Black Jacobins'*.
a) What evidence are we given that African people were forced to participate in the slave trade?
b) What evidence is there that during the Middle Passage slaves would try to escape? What methods were used to prevent slaves from planning escape and rebellion?
c) Find out more information about Toussaint L' Ouverture and the San Domingo Revolution.

(3) **William Mathieson** - *'Great Britain And The Slave Trade'*.
a) Why do you think that it was in the interest of the slave traders to make sure that their "cargo" arrived in good condition?
b) Describe, in your own words, conditions on board a slave ship.
c) What diseases did both slaves and crew risk catching?
d) Find out the names of French, British, Dutch and Spanish Caribbean islands.

(4) **Olaudah Equiano** - from *'Equiano's Travels'*.
a) Teachers should get the class to relax and close their eyes and then read Equiano's account of the Middle Passage. At the end of the account the teacher can ask a number of questions about the details of the story, or simply give pupils and students the opportunity to give their views. The following points should be emphasised:

a) Equiano's age when he was captured. What would the experience of the Middle Passage have really been like for a ten or eleven year old, someone younger than class members (perhaps they could try and write their own account).
b) The fact that Equano had never seen the ocean before; he had never seen a white face before and he had never seen a large ship. What must this have been like?
c) What was Equiano's life like in Africa before he was captured? Equiano says, "I even wished for my former slavery in preference to my present situation".

b) Pupils to carry out research into the life of Equiano. What was his experience like in England travelling around speaking out against slavery? What information is there on his family like in Ely Cambridgeshire?

DESCRIPTION OF THE SLAVE SHIP 'BROOKES'

Teachers to use the illustration of the Brookes and the information from Dicky Sam's *'Liverpool and Slavery'* to reinforce certain details in relation to the Middle Passage, particularly conditions on board ship and the horror and misery of the journey. In terms of the actual space for the slaves on board ship ,the lower decks of the Brookes were about 100ft long. The ship held as many as 600 slaves. Teachers should emphasise the dimensions of the different areas of the Brookes and get pupils to use spaces in the school and classroom as frames of reference to facilitate a better understanding.

The illustration should be used to open up the slavery debate in order to give pupils and students the opportunity to discuss:

> * **the immorality of the slave trade;**
> * **the resilience of the people who survived slavery and the experience of the contemporary disaspora;**
> * **the experiences of those who were the "man stealers". How were they able to participate in such a trade? Could they have had any motives other than economic ones?**

PRELUDE - THE SLAVER

'Prelude - The Slaver' should be used to reinforce the horror of the Middle Passage. As with Equiano's story, pupils and students should read the poem, or have it read to them. Then they can be asked a number of questions in relation to it or be given the opportunity to say how they feel about it. Does the poem capture the true horror, does it reinforce the idea of the *'noble savage'*:

> *"His glance fell on the man who said that he had been a king, the man called*

Tarbarrel, the image of black stone whose eyes were savage gods. The huge suave muscles rippled like stretching cats as he changed posture."

Pupils should be encouraged to write their own account of the Middle Passage in poem form, and as a cross-curricular theme.

PRELUDE - THE SLAVER

The lantern shook his hand.
This was black, here,
This was black to see and feel and smell and taste, the blackness of black, with one weak lamp to light it as ineffectually as a firefly in hell, and, being so, should be silent.
But the hold was never silent.
There was always that breathing.
Always that thick breathing, always those shivering cries.

A few of the slaves knew the English for water and Jesus. "I'm dying. Sick, ..my name is Caesar." Those who knew these things, said these things now when they saw the lantern. Mechanically, as tamed beasts answer the whipcrack.
Their voices beat at the light like heavy moths.
But most made merely liquid or guttural sounds Meaningless to the mate, but horribly like the sound of plateless men or animals trying to talk through a human throat.

The mate was used to the confusion of limbs and bodies by now.
At first it had made him think of their perturbed Blind coil of blacksnakes thawing on a rock in the bleak sun of spring, or Judgment Day just after the first sound of the trump when all earth seethes and crumbles with the slow vast, mouldy resurrection of the dead.
But he had passed such fancies.

He must see as much as he could. He couldn't see very much. They were too tightly packed but no plague yet and the chains were fast. Then he saw something.
The woman was asleep but her baby was dead.
He wondered whether to take it from her now.
No, he would arouse the others. Tomorrow.

He turned with a shiver.
His glance fell on a man who said he had been
king, the man called Tarbarrel, the image of
black stone whose eyes were savage gods.
The huge suave muscles rippled like stretching
cats as he changed posture,
magnificent in chains that yet was ease.
The smoulder in those eyes. The steady hate.

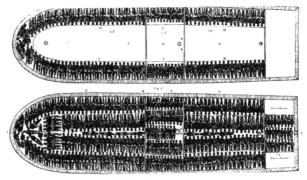

THE SLAVE SHIP 'BROOKES'

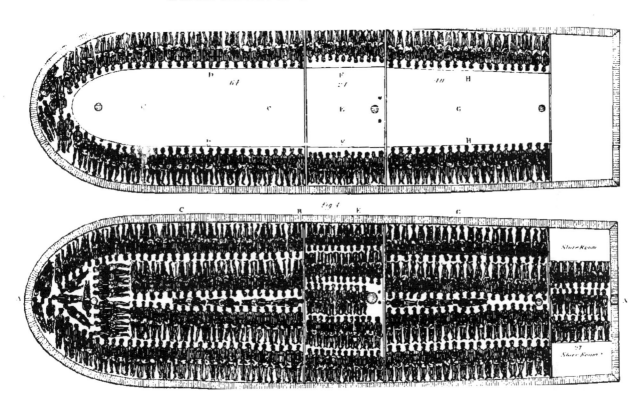

ON BOARD THE 'BROOKES'

   So small was the place allowed to each, they had not so much room as a man in a coffin. They were placed lying on their back, and sometimes they were packed spoonways, one on the other; so close were they, you could not walk without treading on them, but then they were only slaves. One kind hearted sailor, when passing over them, would remove his shoes so as not to hurt them. So close and foul was the stench arising from the negroes, they have been known to be put down the hold strong and healthy at night; and have been dead in the morning. A trader stated that after remaining ten minutes in the hold, his shirt was as wet as if it had been in a bucket of water. What must have been their feelings, the acute pains of these poor wretches, whose only crime was that of colour? As many as 800 have been stowed in the holds of these infernal ships, and to add to their wretchedness, remaining in for a four month voyage to the West Indies; the white man arrogating to himself the supreme privilege of being the lord and master of the blacks; to buy, to sell, to torture, and to kill as he pleases.

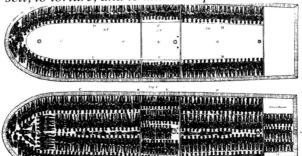

The "Good" Ship
Thomas

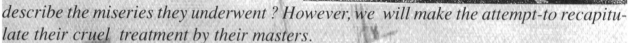

The good ship 'Thomas' got her cargo all safely packed in the hold, and on their passage from Africa to the West Indies. I will here endeavour, and very feebly-for where is the pen or the tongue that can describe the miseries they underwent ? However, we will make the attempt-to recapitulate their cruel treatment by their masters.

When the weather permitted, the slaves were brought up on deck each morning about eight o'clock (except in rough weather when they remained below), they were all chained together by means of ring-bolts fastened to the decks to prevent them from jumping overboard, which many of them would gladly prefer, and some have succeeded in leaping into the sea, which to them was a happy release compared to a miserable life-long slavery. Their meals were composed of raw yams, and horse-beans, which was served out twice daily, with half a pint of water after each meal.

The sickly slaves were scarcely attended to at all; sometimes the captain of the ship would inspect them, and if he found they were likely to give any trouble, he would call two or three of his crew, saying, " I think these niggers had better go overboard, they will leave us more room and help to feed the sharks; I see they are in our track." (The negroes were so often thrown overboard that the course of sharks might be seen for miles watching these ships and waiting for their food).

When feeding time was over, they were called upon to jump, in order to keep them healthy and strong, Jump they could not bound in chains fastened to the deck. The skipper cries out "Jump ! ye niggers; jump!" and, with a cat-o-nine-tails, makes them do his bidding. They now jump as best they can; reports of this healthy exercise were sent home to Liverpool, and they were there told that the negroes were happy and danced for joy. Just imagine; for several days and, perhaps, weeks - which to them seemed like years - closed in, hatches covered, short supplies of water, stifling suffocation of men, women, and children. Do you not hear their groans, their wailings and heavy sighs, but no relief comes. The crew and captain are carousing and making merry, pipes, tobacco, and rum, with lewd songs to cheer them amid the horrible surroundings. And when fine weather comes again, the slaves are made to sing, but their song is a song of sorrow and sadness, the subject matter was their wretched life and loss of their native home for ever.

The captain makes inquiries as to the quantity of water, and it is reported very short. The purser says, " Have been down into the hold this morning, and I should think there are about forty dead niggers, I suppose we had better have them overboard!" To which the captain replies, "Yes, and as soon as you like: hand them up here, more grub for the sharks," and so the negroes are thrown into the sea, one after *another, the captain meanwhile bullying the men, and among the dying negroes are several sailors who have caught the fever, who were dragged on board the ship 'Thomas', of Liverpool, when drunk; a few more days and they will be food for the sharks. Their wives and children at the old home have often prayed for their safe return, but their prayers have not been heard nor answered; the old house will be desolate, and the little ones will have to struggle on in life alone. So what with the feeding of the slaves, their exercise, and their punishment, time wears on. The captain bullies the men, the men torture the slaves, the slaves' hearts are breaking with despair; many more are dead, their bodies thrown into the sea, more food for the sharks; and amid these calamities the ship 'Thomas' arrives safely at Kingston, Jamaica.*

Her lading bill consisted of 630 slaves, of which 100 have died in the horrible middle passage; the ship was soom emptied of her living cargo, they were much worse in condition on landing than when they embarked. It so happened there was a scarcity of slaves in the port when the 'Thomas', of Liverpool, arrived. Captain Roberts obtained prices varying from £50, £60, £70, and in some cases £100 for slaves of special capacities. After a stay of three weeks, the 530 slaves were disposed of, and the vessel once more loaded with specie, sugar and rum. Favourable winds and fine weather accompanied the ship 'Thomas', with her bullying Captain Roberts; some of the crew were lying in the deep or had served as grub for the sharks, but these things are of little moment to the anxious owners of the well-laden ship She might have been seen rushing through the waters like a thing of life. A few days more, and the English coast is sighted, the crew and the captain are in good spirits, nearer and nearer, she makes good headway, now she enters the port of Liverpool. A few hours later and she is safely docked in the same berth which she left twelve months ago. What an eventful voyage it has been-first with her cargo of trumpery trinkets, pistols, muskets, gun- powder, cutlasses, and such like; these bartered for living beings, villages set on fire, wars made between unoffending people, men-stealers prowling about the country, a thousand subterfuges resorted to, in order to kidnap the poor negroes. Women torn from their suckling infants, sons, and daughters from fathers and mothers, and humanity outraged in the name of religion.

From 'Liverpool And Slavery' - Dicky Sam

Olaudah Equiano's Story

Equiano, an 11 year old, has been captured and transported to the coast. He describes his thoughts and feelings as he catches sight of a slave ship.

The first object which saluted my eyes when I arrived on the coast was the sea, and a slave ship, which was then riding at anchor, and waiting for its cargo. These filled me with astonishment, which was soon converted into terror when I was carried on board. I was immidiately handled and tossed up to see if I were sound by some of the crew; and I was now persuaded that I had gotten into a world of bad spirits, and that they were going to kill me. Their complexions too differing so much from ours, their long hair, and the language they spoke, (which was very different from any I had ever heard) united to confirm me in this belief. Indeed such were the horrors of my view and fears at the moment, that, if ten thousand worlds had been my own, I would have freely parted with them all to have exchanged my condition with that of the meanest slave in my own country. When I looked round the ship too and saw a large furnace or copper boiling and a multitude of black people of every description chained together every one of their countenances expressing dejection and sorrow, I no longer doubted of my fate; and, quite overpowered with horror and anguish, I fell motionless on the deck and fainted. When I recovered a little I found some black people about me, who I believed were some of those who brought me on board, and had been receiving their pay. They talked to me in order to cheer me, but all in vain. I asked them if we were not to be eaten by those white men with horrible looks, red faces, and loose hair. They told me I was not; and one of the crew brought me a small portion of spiritous liquor in a wine glass; but being afraid of him, I would not take it out of his hand. One of the blacks therefore took it from him and gave it to me, and I took a little down my palate, which, instead of reviving me, as they thought it threw me into the greatest constenation at the strange feeling it produced, having never tasted any such liquor before. Soon after this the blacks who brought me on board went off, and left me abandoned to despair. I now saw myself deprived of all chance of returning to my native country, or even the least glimpse of hope of gaining the shore, which I now considered as friendly; and I even wishcd for my former slavery in preference to my present situation which was filled with horrors of every kind, still heightened by my ignorance of what I was to undergo.

I was not long suffered to indulge my grief; I was soon put down under the decks, and there I received such a salutation in my nostrils as I had never experienced in my life: so that, with the loathsomeness of the stench, and crying together, became so sick and low that I was not able to eat, nor had I the least desire to taste anything.

95

I now wished for the last friend, death, to relieve me; but soon, to my grief, two of the white men offered me eatables; and, on my refusing to eat, one of them held me fast by the hands, and laid me across I think the windlass, and tied my feet, while the other flogged me severely. I had never experienced any thing of this kind before; and although, not being used to the water, naturally feared that element the first time

vived, and thought, if it were no worse than working, my situation was not so desperate: but still I feared I should be put to death, the white people looked and acted, as I thought, in so savage a manner; for I had never seen among any people such instances of brutal cruelty; and this not only shewn towards us blacks but also to some of the whites themselves. One white man in particular I saw, when we were permitted to be on deck, flogged so unmercifully with a large rope near the foremast, that he died in consequence of it and they tossed him over the side as they would have done a brute. This made me fear these people the more; and expected nothing less than to be treated in the same manner. I could not help expressing my fears and apprehensions to some of my countrymen: I asked them if these people had no country, but lived in this hollow place (the ship): they told me they did not, but came from a distant one. "Then" said I, "how comes it in all our country we never heard of them?" They told me because they lived so very far off. I then added where were their women? had they any like themselves? I was told they had: "And why", said I, "do we not see them?" They answered, because they were left behind. I asked how the vessel could go? They told me they could not tell; but that there were cloths upon the masts by the help of the

I saw it, yet nevertheless could I have got over the nettings, I would have jumped over the side but I could not; and, besides, the crew used to watch us very close who were not chained down to the decks, lest we should leap into the water: and I have seen some of these poor African prisoners most severely cut for attempting to do so, and hourly whipped for not eating. This indeed was often the case with myself. In a little time after, amongst the poor chained men, I found some of my own nation, which in a small degree gave ease to my mind. I inquired of these what was to be done with us; they gave me to understand we were to be carried to these white people's country to work for them. Then I was a little re-

ropes I saw, and then the vessel was on; and the white men had some spell or magic they put in the water when they liked in order to stop the vessel. I was exceedingly amazed at this account, and really thought they were spirits. I therefore wished much to be from amongst them, for I expected they would sacrifice me: but my wishes were vain; for we were so quartered that it was impossible for any of us to make our escape. While we stayed off the coast I was mostly on deck; and one day, to my great astonishment, I saw one of these vessels coming in with the sails up. As soon as the whites saw it, they gave a great shout, at which we were amazed; and the more so as the vessel appeared larger by approaching nearer.

At last she came to an anchor in my sight, and when the anchor was let go I and my

countrymen who saw it were lost in astonishment to observe the vessel stop; and were now convinced it was done by magic. Soon after this the other ship got her boats out and they came on board of us, and the people of both ships seemed very glad to see each other. Several of the strangers also shook hands with us black people, and made motions with their hands, signifying I suppose we were to go to their country; but we did not understand them. At last, when the ship we were in had got in all her cargo, they made ready with many fearful noises, and we were all put under the deck, so that we could not see how they managed the vessel. But this disappointment was the least of my sorrow. The stench of the hold while we were on the coast was so intolerably loathsome, that it was dangerous to remain there for any time, and some of us had been permitted to stay on the deck for the fresh air; but now that the whole ships cargo were confined together, it became absolutely pestilential. The closeness of the place, and the heat of the climate, added to the number in the ship, which was so crowded that each had scarcely room to turn himself, almost suffocated us. This produced copious perspirations, so that the air soon became unfit for respiration, from variety of loathsome smells, and brought on a sickness among the slaves, of which many died, thus falling victims to the improvident avarice, as I may call it, of their purchasers. This wretched situation was again aggravated by the galling of the chains, now became insupportable; and the filth of the necessary tubs, into which the children often fell, and were almost suffocated. The shrieks of the women, and the groans of the dying, rendered the whole a scene of horror almost inconceivable. Happily perhaps for myself I was soon reduced so low and from my extreme youth I was not put in fetters. In this situation I expected every hour to share the fate of my companions, some of whom were almost daily brought upon deck at the point of death which I began to hope would soon put an end to my miseries. Often did I think many of the inhabitants of the deep much more happy than myself. I envied them the freedom they enjoyed, and as often wished I could change my condition for theirs. Every circumstance met with served only to render my state more painful, and heighten my apprehensions, and my opinion of the cruelty of the whites. One day they had taken a number of fishes; and when they had killed and satisfied themselves with as many as they thought fit, to our astonishment who were on the deck, rather than give any of them to us to eat as we expected, they tossed the remaining fish into the sea again although we begged and prayed for some as well as we could, but in vain; and some of my countrymen, being pressed by hunger, took an opportunity, when they thought no one saw them, of trying to get a little privately; but they were discovered, and the attempt procured them some very severe floggings.

One day, when we had a smooth sea and moderate wind, two of my wearied countrymen who were chained together (I was near them at the time), preferring death to such a life of misery, somehow made through the nettings and jumped into the sea: immediately another quite dejected fellow, who, on account of his illness, was suffered to be out of irons, also followed their example; and I believe many more would very soon have done the same if they had not been prevented by the ship's crew, who were instantly alarmed. Those of us that were the most active were in a moment put down under the deck, and there was such a noise and confusion amongst the people of the ship as I never heard before, to stop her, and get the boat out to go after the slaves. However two of the wretches were drowned, but they got the other, and afterwards flogged him unmercifully for thus attempting to prefer death to slavery. In
this manner we continued to undergo more hardships than I can now relate, hardships which are inseparable from this accursed trade. Many a time we were near suffocation from the want of fresh air, which we were often without for whole days together. This, and the stench of the necessary tubs, carried off many. During our passage I first saw flying fishes, which surprised me very much: they used frequently to fly across the ship, and many of them fell on the deck. I also now first saw the use of the quadrant; I had often with astonishment seen the mariners make observations with it, and I could not think what it meant.

They at last took notice of my surprise and one of them, willing to increase it, as well as to gratify my curiosity, made me one day look through it. The clouds appeared to me to be land, which disappeared as they passed along. This heightend my wonder; and I was now more persuaded than ever that I was in another world, and that every thing about me was magic. At last we came in sight of the island of Barbadoes, at which the whites on board gave a great shout, and made many signs of joy to us. We did not know what to think of this; but as the vessel drew nearer plainly saw the harbour, and other ships of different kinds and size and we soon anchored amongst them off Bridge Town. Man merchants and planters now came on board, though it was in the evening. They put us in separate parcels, and examined us attentively. They also made us jump, and pointed to the land, signifying we were to go there. We thought by this we should be eaten by these ugly men, as they appeared to us; and, when soon after we were all put down under the deck again, there was much dread and trembling among us, and nothing but bitter cries to be heard all the night from these apprehensions, insomuch that at last the white people got some old slaves from the land to pacify us. They told us we were not to be eaten, but to work, and were soon to go on land, where we should see many of our country people. This report eased us much; and sure enough, soon after we were landed, there came to us Africans of many languages. We were conducted immediately to the merchant's yard where we were all pent up together like so many sheep in a fold without regard to sex or age. As every object was new to me every thing I saw filled me with surprise. What struck me first was that the houses were built with stones, and in every other respect different from those in Africa: but I was still more astonished on seeing people on horseback. I did not know what this could mean; and indeed I thought these people were full of nothing but magical arts.

Olaudah Equiano from 'Equiano's Travels'.

CLR James - From , 'The Black Jacobins'.

THE SLAVERS scoured the coasts of Guinea. As they devastated an area they moved westward and then south, decade after decade, past the Niger, down the Congo coast, past Loango and Angola, round the Cape of Good Hope, and, by 1789. even as far as Mozambique on the eastern side of Africa. Guinea remained their chief hunting ground. From the coast they organised expeditions far into the interior. They set the simple tribesmen fighting against each other with modern weapons over thousands of square miles. The propagandists of the time claimed that however cruel was the slave traffic, the African slave in America was happier than in his own African civilisation.

Ours, too, is an age of propaganda. We excel our ancestors only in system and organisation: they lied as fluently and as brazenly. In the sixteenth century, Central Africa was a territory of peace and happy civilisation. Traders travelled thousands of miles from one side of the continent to another without molestation. The tribal wars from which the European pirates claimed to deliver the people were mere sham-fights; it was a great battle when half-a-dozen men were killed. It was on a peasantry in many respects superior to the serfs in large areas of Europe, that the slave-trade fell. Tribal life was broken up and millions of detribalised Africans were let loose upon each other. The unceasing destruction of crops led to cannibalism; the captive women became concubines and degraded the status of the wife. Tribes had to supply slaves or be sold as slaves themselves. Violence and ferocity became the necessities for survival, and violence and ferocity survived. The stockades of grinning skulls, the human sacrifices, the selling of their own children as slaves, these horrors were the product of an intolerable pressure on the Arican peoples, which became fiercer through the centuries as the demands of industry increased and the methods of coercion were perfected.

The slaves were collected in the interior, fastened one to the other in columns, loaded with heavy stones of 40 or 50 pounds in weight to prevent attempts at escape, and then marched the long journey to the sea, sometimes hundreds of miles, the weakly and sick dropping to die in the African jungle. Some were brought to the coast by canoe, lying in the bottom of boats for days on end, their hands bound, their faces exposed to the tropical sun and the tropical rain, their backs in the water which was never bailed out. At the slave ports they were penned into "trunks" for the inspection of the buyers. Night and day thousands of human beings were packed in these "dens of putrefaction" so that no European could stay in them for longer than a quarter of an hour without fainting. The Africans fainted and recovered or fainted and died, the mortality in the "trunks" being over 20 per cent. Outside in the harbour, waiting to empty the "trunks" as they filled, was the captain of the slave-ship, with so clear a conscience *that one of them, in the intervals of waiting to enrich British capitalism with the profits of another valuable cargo, enriched British religion by composing the hymn* **"How Sweet the Name of Jesus Sounds."**

On the ships the slaves were packed in the hold on galleries one above the other. Each was given only four or five feet in length and two or three feet in height, so that they could neither lie at full length nor sit upright. Contrary to the lies that have been spread so pertinaciously about Negro docility, the revolts at the port of embarkation and on board were incessant, so that the slaves had to be chained, right hand to right leg, left hand to left leg, and attached in rows to long iron bars. In this position they lived for the voyage, coming up once a day for exercise and to allow the sailors to "clean the pails." But when the cargo was rebellious or the weather bad, then they stayed below for weeks at a time. The close proximity of so many naked human beings, their bruised and festering flesh, the foetid air, the prevailing dysentery, the accumulation of filth, turned these holds into a hell. During the storms the hatches were battened down, and in the close and loathsome darkness they were hurled from one side to another by the heaving vessel, held in position by the chains on their bleeding flesh. No place on earth, observed one writer of the time, concentrated so much misery as the hold of a slave-ship.

Twice a day, at nine and at four, they received their food. To the slave-traders they were articles of trade and no more. A captain held up by calms or adverse winds was known to have poisoned his cargo. Another killed some of his slaves to feed tne others with the flesh. They died not only from the regime but from grief and rage and despair. They undertook vast hunger strikes; undid their chains and hurled themselves on the crew in futile attempts at insurrection. What could these inland tribesmen do on the open sea, in a complicated sailing vessel? To brighten their spirits it became the custom to have them up on the deck once a day and force them to dance. Some took the opportunity to jump overboard, uttering cries of triumph as they cleared the vessel and disappeared below the surface.

Fear of their cargo bred a savage cruelty in the crew. One captain, to stike terror into the rest, killed a slave and dividing heart, liver and entrails into 3oo pieces made each of the slaves eat one, threatening those who refused with the same torture. Such incidents were not rare. Given the circumstances such things were (and are) inevitable. Nor did the system spare the slavers. Every year one-fifth of all who took part in the African trade died. ..... When the ship reached the harbour, the cargo came up on deck to be bought. ....Having become the property of his owner, he was branded on both sides of the breast with a hot iron. His duties were explained to him by an interpreter, and a priest instructed him in the first principles of Christianity.

CLR James From 'The Black Jacobins'.

101

William Mathieson 'Great Britain And The Slave Trade'

It has often been said that the importer of a perishable cargo, whether negroes or cattle, must have wished in his own interest that it should arrive in good condition, but the slave-trader in all ages had subordinated quality to bulk. Knowing that disease might lurk amongst his victims, however well chosen, he thought it the best policy to have a wide margin against loss, and there were sanatoriums, as they would now be called, in which the emaciated, dazed and staggering creatures who emerged from the hold of a slaver were recuperated for sale. Thus the slaves were always packed, often so closely that they sat between each other's legs; they were chained by the ankle in pairs, their fetters being, not locked, but riveted; and the boarding above them was in many cases so low that they could not even sit upright. The bent back frequently stiffened; and at Sierra Leone could be seen "liberated slaves in every conceivable state of distortion." In the smaller vessels, the decks of which were almost as crowded as their holds, most of the negroes were kept below during the whole voyage of a month or six weeks. The stench arising from bad air and the accumulation of filth was overpowering; the bruising of naked and manacled bodies with the rolling and pitching of the ship in a rough sea was an added torment, especially where, as often happened, there was no slave isolation practised in an outbreak of small pox, is indicated by a British naval officer, who said that he found the sick men, women and children thrown together in a heap. "They appeared on looking down to be one living mass. You could hardly tell arms from legs or one person from another or what they were."

The usual diseases were fever and dysentery, but a mysterious sort of ophthalmia was not uncommon; and in the notorious case of the 'Rodeur', a French slaver of 1819, every person on board except one seaman became more or less blind. When the vessel reached Guadeloupe, this man reported that he had seen and hailed a large Spanish slaver which was drifting to destruction in charge of a sightless crew. The worst agony was that of thirst, water being always scarce, at all events in proportion to the feverish demand. One who visited a prize on its arrival at Sierra Leone describes the slaves as " in a profuse state of perspiration and panting like so many hounds for air and water." In 1831 a Spanish slave-ship was chased and overtaken off Fernando Po by a famous cruiser called, the 'Black Joke'. Though much better armed and manned, she was boarded after several hours' fighting; and the captors were astonished at the "headlong eagerness" of the negroes when offered a liberal supply of water. "Their heads became wedged in the tub and were with some difficulty got out"; the drops that fell on the deck were *eagerly lapped up; and, when jugs were handed round, " they madly bit the vessels with their teeth and champed them into atoms." Female slaves, though always the most difficult to manage on the plantations are said to have borne their sufferings more quietly than the men, who frequently fought with each other or committed suicide; but they brooded, and many of them and these the most lively and intelligent became insane.*

..... The extent of the slave trade could be estimated only from the number of its victims actually landed in the importing countries but, as Lord John Russell said, "No record exists of the multitudes who perish on the overland journey to the African coast, or in the passage across the Atlantic, or of the still greater number who fall a sacrifice to the warfare, pillage and cruelties by which the slave trade is fed." The general calculation was that, of the slaves captured in the interior, one-third perished in the journey, another third in the barracoons, where they were collected for exportation, and on the voyage, and only the remaining third lived to become labourers on the plantations.

THE CASE OF THE 'ZONG'

Of all the recorded horrors of the Atlantic slave trade, perhaps the most appalling is that of the slave ship 'Zong', whose master, Luke Collingwood, threw 132 slaves overboard to collect the insurance. Its significance was two-fold. Firstly it exemplified the extreme barbarities of the trade, and secondly, when the facts became known, it was adopted as a test case by the English abolitionist, Granville Sharpe, to show the inhumanities of English law. The incident occurred in September 1781. Granville Sharpe heard about it only two years later when the claim by the owners against the insurers came to court. He

was told of the incident by the former slave and anti-slavery activist, Olaudah Equiano. His account runs as follows:

"19th March 1783 Vassa (Equiqno) called on me with an account of 132 negroes being thrown alive into the sea, from on board an English slave-ship. The circumstances of this case could not fail to excite a deep interest. The master of a slave-ship trading from Africa to Jamaica, and having 440 slaves on board, had thought fit, on a pretext that he might be distressed on his voyage for want of water, to lessen the consumption of' it in the vessel, by throwing overboard 132 of the most sick among the slaves. On his return to England, the owners of the ship claimed from the insurers the full value of those drowned slaves, on the ground that there was an absolute necessity for throwing them into the sea, in order to save the remaining crew, and the ship itself.

The underwriters contested the existence of the alleged necessity; or, if it had existed, attributed it to the ignorance and improper conduct of the master of the vessel. This contest of pecuniary interest brought to light a scene of horrid brutality which had been acted during the execution of a detestable plot. From the trial it appeared that the ship Zong, Luke Collingwood master, sailed from the island of St Thomas, on the Coast of Africa, 6 September 1781, with 440 slaves and fourteen whites on board, for Jamaica, and that in the November following she fell in with that island; but instead of proceeding to some port, the master, mistaking, as he alleges, Jamaica for Hispaniola, ran her to leeward. Sickness and mortality had by this time taken place on board the crowded vessel: so that, between the time of leaving the coast of Africa and the 9th of November, sixty slaves and seven white people had died;and a great number of the surviving slaves were then sick and not likely to live . On that day the master of the ship called together a few of the officers, and stated to them, that, if the sick slaves died a natural death, the loss would fall on the owners of the ship; but, if they were thrown alive into the sea, on any sufficient pretext of necessity for the safety of the ship, it would be the loss of the underwriters, alleging, at the same time, that it would be less cruel to throw sick wretches into the sea, than to suffer them to linger out a few days under the disorder with which they were afflicted.

103

To this inhuman proposal the mate, James Kelsal, at first objected; but Collingwood at length prevailed on the crew to listen to it. He then chose out from the cargo 232 slaves and brought them on

deck, all or most of whom were sickly, and not likely to recover, and he ordered the crew by turns to throw them into the sea. 'A parcel' of them were accordingly thrown overboard, and, on counting over the remainder the next morning, it appeared that the number so drowned had been fifty- four. He then ordered another parcel to be thrown over, which, on a second counting on the succeeding day was proved to have amounted to forty-two.

On the third day the remaining thirty six were brought on deck, and, as these now resisted the cruel purpose of their masters, the arms of twenty-six were fettered with irons, and the savage crew proceeded with the diabolical work, casting them down to join their comrades of the former days. Outraged misery could endure no longer; the ten last victims sprang distainfully from the grasp of their tyrants, defied their power, and leaping into the sea, felt a momentary triumph in the face of death."

The owners of the Zong claimed the full value of the slaves, £30 each, from the insurers, on the grounds that there was an absolute necessity to throw them into the sea in order to save the lives of the crew. The necessity given was the scarcity of water. But no one on the ship had been short of a water allowance, and when the ship arrived in Jamaica it had on board 420 gallons of water to spare. The absolute necessity was Collingwoods greed, for it had already been established in English law that:

"The insurer takes upon him the risk of the loss, capture, and death of slaves, or any other unavoidable accident to them: but natural death is always understood to be expected: by natural death is meant , not only when it happens by disease or sickness , but also when the captive distroys himself through dispair, which often happens: but when slaves are killed ... to quell an insurrection.... then the insurers must answer."

The legal battle that ensued after the case of the Zong raised many legal and ethical questions about the cuelty and injustice of slavery and the slave trade. Although the owners of the Zong won their legal battle for compensation for ***"loss of goods"***, it was overturned on appeal.

REFERENCES
Susanne Everette 'The Slaves - An
Illustrated History of The Monstrouse Evil.
Bison Books Ltd 1978.

BACKGROUND IMAGES:
Page 93 a slave ship; page 98 Equiano and page 103, slaves being thrown over board.

LIVERPOOL, THE SLAVE TRADE AND SLAVE TRADERS

Exercises , Learning Materials And Activities

Clearance To The Coast Of Africa

A) Teachers to give information to pupils and students on the dates that Liverpool became involved in the slave trade and some indication of how local slave traders benefited and developed their interests. Teachers should point out that Liverpool was last in, compared to London and Bristol, and last out of the slave trade.

B) Pupils and students to be given the table showing the clearance of ships to Africa from Bristol, Liverpool and London (page 112) and asked to draw information in graph form.

C) Teachers should then ask the following:

* *What general trends emerge from the graphs?*
* *Why was Liverpool slow to participate in the slave trade? What evidence do you have to support your answer?*
* *It may be that the evidence presented in your graph is not completely accurate. For what reasons might slave captains have falsified their records?*

THE SLAVE TRADERS

1) Teachers to give copies of *'Name of Street - Origins of Name'* tables (pp106-107) to pupils and students and ask a number of questions in relation to them. For example:

* *Who were the slave traders?*
* *Did they have political and eco-*nomic power? If so, how were they able to use their power and influence to support their economic interests?

2) Teachers to prepare an outline map of the city. Pupils and students to locate street names on the map. Teachers should ask the following questions in relation to the exercise:

* *In which part of the city are the streets located?*
* *Most of the streets are located in a small geographical area. What does this tell us about the city?*

ADDITIONAL RESEARCH

* *What conclusions can we draw from the fact that streets, buildings, monuments, districts etc. were named after people who were directly involved in the slave trade?*
* *Take two names from the list of slave merchants and carry out further research into their lives. Include in your research details about their political activities, family life and how they sought to protect their trading interests (see Johnson, Cunliffe, Tarleton and Gildart for further information pp 110-111).*
* *Find out more information about slave traders not mentioned in this section.*
* *Visit the Town Hall and take the names of the Lord Mayors of Liverpool from 1740 to 1807. How many of them were involved in slavery?*

Find out more information about street names, for example:

* *What streets are there naming countries which were either part of the Triangular Trade, or connected with the British Empire?*
* *From what writers have said there were streets in Liverpool which were associated with Black people; Negro Row is an example. Find out if there are any streets named after Black people. Blackmoor Drive may be an example. Find out the origin of the term "Blackmoor", or "Blackamoore".*

NAME OF STREET	ORIGINS OF NAME
(1) Ashton Street	The Ashton family. Amongst its memhers was the slave-trading merchant John Ashton.
(2) Atherton Street	The Atherton family. Amongst its members was the slave-trading merchant John Atherton.
(3) Bamber Street	Bamber Gascoyne. A Liverpool MP who defended the slave trade in Parliament.
(4) Banastre Street	Banastre Tarleton. A Liverpool MP who defended the slave trade in Parliament.
(5) Blackburne Place	John Blackburne, a Liverpool slave-trading merchant .
(6) Bold Street	Jonas Bold, a Liverpool slave-trading merchant.
(7) Brooks Alley	Joseph and Johnathon Brooks, Liverpool slave-trading merchants.
(8) Campbell Street	George Campbell, a Liverpool merchant who dealt in slave-produced West Indian sugar.
(9) Clarence Street	The Duke of Clarence, who spoke in Parliament in defence of the slave trade.
(10) Cunliffe Street	Foster Cunliffe, a Liverpool slave-trading merchant.
(11) Dorans Lane	Felix Doran, a Liverpool slave-trading merchant.
(12) Earle Road	The Earle family, Liverpool slave-trading merchants.
(13) Gascoyne Street	Isaac Gascoyne. A Liverpool MP who defended the slave trade in Parliament.
(14) Gildart Gardens and Gildart Street	Richard Gildart, a Liverpool slave-trading merchant.

(15) Hardman Street	The widow of John Hardman a Liverpool slave trading merchant.
(16) Lord Nelson Street	Lord Nelson, naval hero and champion of the slave trade.
(17) Maryland Street	Named in recognition of the importance of the slave produced tobacco for the Liverpool economy.
(18) Oldham Street	James Oldham, a Liverpool slaving captain.
(19) Parr Street	The Parr family. Amongst its members were the slave trading merchants John and Edward Parr.
(20) Rathbone Road	The Rathbone family. Two members of the family were abolitionists, but their principle service to Liverpool was to initiate the importation of American slave produced cotton.
(21) Rodney Street	Admiral Rodney, naval hero and champion of slavery and the slave trade.
(22) Seel Street	Thomas Seel, a Liverpool slave trading merchant.
(23) Sir Thomas Street & Johnson St.	Sir Thomas Johnson, a pioneering Liverpool slave trading merchant.
(24) Virginia Street	Named in recognition of the importance of slave produced tobacco for the Liverpool economy.
(25) Tarleton Street	The Tarleton family, Liverpool slave trading merchants.

LIVERPOOL SLAVE TRADERS AND STREET NAMES

CAMPBELL STREET L1

BLACKBURNE PLACE L8

OLDHAM STREET

BLACKMOOR DRIVE L12

TRUEMAN STREET

JOHNSON STREET L3

RATHBONE ROAD 13

TARLETON STREET

EARLE STREET L3

CANNING PLACE L1

BOLD STREET L1

THE GOREE L2

GASCOYNE ST. 3.

CLARENCE STREET
BLACKBURNE PLACE
ASHTON STREET
CUNLIFFE
EET L2
SEEL STREET
PARR STREET L1
MARYLAND STREET
HNSON
REET L3
LORD NELSON STREET L3
EARLE STREET
RODNEY STREET L1
HARDMAN STREET
SIR THOMAS STREET L1

Sir Thomas Johnson

*Sir Thomas Johnson described as "The founder of modern Liverpool." He was part owner of the **'Blessing'**, one of the first Liverpool ships to take part in the African slave trade in the early 1700s. He was a pioneering Liverpool merchant who was Lord Mayor in 1695 and sat as M.P. from 1701 to 1723. In 1708 he was knighted. Both Sir Thomas, and Johnson Streets are named after him. (Painting, Walker Art Gallery - National Museums & Galleries on Merseyside).*

Banastre Tarleton

Robert Cunliffe

For over two generations slave-trading merchants dominated the social and political life of Liverpool. Thirty seven out of 41 members of the Liverpool Council in 1787 were involved in the slave trade in one way or another, as too were all 20 Mayors who held office between 1787 and 1807. With the exception of William Roscoe in the period 1806 -1807, all of Liverpool's Members of Parliament in the eighteenth and early nineteenth century were either slave traders in their own right or defended the slave trade in Parliament. *"Liverpool was not just the economic capital of the slave trade, it was the political capital."* (From Cameron and Cooke).

Banastre Tarleton (1754 - 1833) was Lieutenant Colonel commanding the British Legion. He was known as *" Bloody Tarleton "* and designated a butcher and barbarian. He was an advocate of the slave trade in support of major Liverpool interests.

The Tarleton family were steeped in slavery over several generations. Tarleton's father, John, was elected Mayor in 1764 and was the major capital-holder in a company of merchants trading to Africa. He was also one of the most important supplies of slaves to both the American colonies and the Caribbean. There are streets named after both Banastre and the Tarleton family; Banastre and Tarleton streets.

Richard Gildart

Robert Cunliffe was a leading Liverpool merchant. With his father Foster, and his brother Ellis, he part-owned at least 26 ships in the mid 1700s. At least four of these ships: the *'Bulkeley'*, the *'Bridget'*, *'Foster'* and the *'Ellis & Robert'* were slave ships. Altogether these four ships held 1120 slaves, and they brought the Cunliffe family enough profit to load a dozen ships every year with sugar and rum for sale in England.

Robert Cunliffe was born in 1719, the younger son of Foster Cunliffe, a Liverpool M.P. and three times Lord Mayor (1716, 1729 and 1735). Cunliffe street is named after the family.

Richard Gildart (1673/4 - 1770) was a Liverpool merchant in the Virginia Traders and Sugar Refiners. He was a prominent figure in the slave trade in the 1750s. He was a bailiff in1712, Lord Mayor from 1714-15, 1731-32 and 1776-77. He was a Member of Parliament for Liverpool in 1735-54 and Alderman by 1766. Gildart Gardens and Gildart Street are named after him.

LIVERPOOL, CAPITAL OF THE SLAVE TRADE

By the 1740s Liverpool had overtaken both London and Bristol, and established itself as country's most important slave-trading port.

"So early as the year 1744 she (Liverpool) employ more than one half of the vessels engaged in that branch of commerce, the slave trade, and imported annually from Africa more than one half of the slaves purchased by all vessels of Great Britain.....The number of slave clearances for Africa from Liverpool continued to grow in subsequent years. 53 vessels sailed for Africa from Liverpool in 1751, 69 vessels in 1761 and 107 in 1771. By the 1780s there were nearly twice as many slaving vessels clearing from Liverpool each year as the were from Bristol and London combined. Three out of every four slaves shipped to Jamaica in this decade were carried on Liverpool ships, and all but three of the 19 most important British firms engaged in slave trading were based in Livepool." From Cameron and Cooke 'Liverpool Capital of The Slave Trade'. The table below shows the number of clearances to the coast of Africa from the three main British slave trading ports: Liverpool, London and Bristol.

YEAR	CLEARANCES TO THE COAST OF AFRICA			
	LIVERPOOL	BRISTOL	LONDON	TOTAL
1710	2	20	24	46
1725	21	63	87	171
1730s	21	39	35	95
1750 (Annual Average)	49	20	13	82
1771 (Annual Average)	107	23	58	188
CLEARANCES OF SLAVING VESSELS				
	LIVERPOOL	BRISTOL	LONDON	TOTAL
1789	61	33		94
1794	110	31		141
1798	149	11		160
1802	122	33		155
1795-1804 (TOTAL)	1099	184		1283

THE ABOLITION OF THE SLAVE TRADE

Teachers should supply pupils and students with a condensed version of the information presented on this section in Part One. They should be encouraged to carry out further research (see bibliography). The main aim of this section is to explore the various positions with reference to the abolition of the slave trade and to consider the role that Black people played in their own liberation. This section explores the role of Black people as abolitionists and as leaders of rebellions and uprisings.

THE ABOLITION OF THE SLAVE TRADE

a) What are the various explanations of the abolition of slavery? Your answer should be detailed, in the form of a short essay, and it should take into account the following:

✔ *economic reasons;*
✔ *moral reasons;*
✔ *legal explanation - legislation;*
✔ *revolution;*
✔ *problems in plantation societies;*
✔ *religious explanations.*

b) Read through the details presented on the Somerset case and explain its significance (page 39)
c) Find out more about the life of Sojournor Truth and Harriet Tubman and others mentioned in the *'Leaders in Thought and Action'* fact file. (page 115) How did they make the horrors of slavery known to the public and what impact did they have?
d) Carry out research and find out more about the abolitionists. Particular attention should be

paid to Black Abolitionists such as Olaudah Equiano. (page 95-99) Also find out more about William Roscoe and William Wilberforce. Pupils and students should be encouraged to visit the Willberforce Museum in Hull and the Trans-Atlantic Slavery Gallery in the Maritime Museum in Liverpool.

FACT FILE

e) Find out the meaning of the following words: * *revolt;* * *rebellion;* * *revolution;* * *underground railroad;* * *abolition.* Also find out the dates of the main revolutions in the Caribbean. List them and carry out further research.

IMAGES OF ABOLITION

f) Through examining the figures 1-10 pupils and students should be able to say what all of the images have in common. They should also be able to say something about the group responsible for producing them.
g) From a close reading of the images it is possible to tell which society produced them. Do you think that it was Black slaves themselves, the abolitionists, the church or some other group or individual ? Explain your answer.
h) In two of the pictures we see images of Britannia. What do you think the significance of this is? Examine, in detail, picture eight and explains the following:

✔ *who are the three women?*
✔ *who is the bust of?*
✔ *what kind of ship is featured?*
✔ *what is the significance of the lion.*

Pupils should be encouraged to work through the issues in this section in more detail. They should do this through exploring the abolition of slavery as a cross-curricular theme through English and Art.

FACT FILE

First recorded slaving voyage from England. Jack Hawkins departed from the coast of England in 1562.

Dates in the Abolitionists' Calendar - England

* 1787 the Society for the Abolition of the Slave Trade was founded. Society for the Gradual Abolition of Slavery founded under the leadership of Fowell Buxton. Agency committee formed; they changed the policy of gradual abolition. Finally in 1808 the trade in slaves ends.

* 1833 Parliament passed a law to end slavery in the British Colonies. The Emancipation Act is passed: children aged six and under to be freed Immediately; domestic slaves serve an appreticeship of four years, field slaves to serve for a period of six years; owners to receive 20 million pounds in compensation.

Dates in the American Abolitionistss calendar

* 1833 the American Anti-Slavery Society formed, this has a broad based Black and white membership.

* 1836 Gag Resolution passed by Congress, effectively prohibiting the issue of slavery from being discussed.

* 1840 American Foreign Anti - Slavery Society formed: focus is put on political action. Both anti-slavery societies form associations with free Blacks.

* 1850 Missouri Compromise. New states joining the Union had to decided whether to be slave holding or not.

* 1854 Kansas Nebraska Act. People in these territories had to decide whether to hold slaves or not. The formation of a new Republican Party aimed to halt the spread of slavery. Lincoln is elected in 1860.

* Southern States break away from the Northern States in February 1861 - war broke out in April.

* 1861 the need for more troops forced Lincoln to issue the Emancipation Proclamation on January 1st 1863. 1865 the Civil War ended.

Dates in the Caribbean Abolitionist calendar

* Haitian Revolution 1791 - 95. Enslaved Africans in the French colony, St. Domingo (Haiti) defeated the power of the British and the French armies. 1804 St. Domingo became known as Haiti.

* August 1st 1834: the abolition of slavery came into effect in the British West Indies. This date is celebrated in the Caribbean as Emancipation Day.

Important Legal Cases England

* **The 'Zong'.** In 1781 Captain Luke Collingwood ordered 131 slaves to be thrown overboard. The ship Zong owned by a Liverpool slaving company was heading for Jamaica. Colingwood told his officers **" ... if slaves died a natural death, it would be the loss of the owners of the ship; but if they were thrown alive into the sea it would be the loss of the underwriters."** When the case came to court public sympathies were aroused and a significant boost was given to the abolitionists' case.

* **Somerset Case.** On the 22nd of May 1772 Lord Mansfield declared the judgment that : **"As soon as a slave set foot on the soil of the British Islands, he became free."** This was seen by some commentators as the beginnings of the abolition of slavery. Somerset was an enslaved African who escaped from the Caribbean to England.

Important Legal Cases - America.

* **L'Amistad.** 1839 slaves revolted and seized a Spanish slaver which was travelling in between Cuban ports. Led by an African slave known as Cinque, the slaves tried to return to Africa but the Europeans steered them to Long Shore Island in New York. The abolitionists won the case for the freedom of the men on the L' Amistad in the US Supreme Court and the slaves were sent back to Africa. The sole Cuban born slave had to escape by using the **'Underground Railroad'.**

114

LEADERS IN THOUGHT
AND ACTION

Harriet Tubman. *Born into slavery in 1823 and known as "the Moses of her people" she was the underground railroad's best known conductor. Tubman escaped from Maryland in 1849 and helped an estimated 300 slaves to escape. Slave holders offered $20,000 dollars for Tubman's capture. Tubman never received a pension for her civil war work.*

Sojournor Truth. *1790 - 1883. Formerly known as Isabella Baumfree. Born a slave in 1790 she escaped, changed her name to Sojourner Truth, and joined movements for freedom and women's rights. Sojourner Truth delivered her most famous speech 'Ain't I A Woman?' in 1852 at an Ohio women's rights convention.*

James Forten. *1746 - 1842. Born a freeman in Philadelphia he made a living servicing ships in his own dry dock. Forten opposed the state of Philadelphia's attempt to stop free Blacks from moving there. He was an opponent of colonisation. Forten met with Garrison to found the American Anti- Slavery Society in 1832.*

Phyliss Wheatley. *America's first Black poet. Brought by the Wheatley family out of Boston in 1761 she mastered English and Latin. She died penniless and alone in 1774. Phyliss Wheatley came to England and Wales as a result of her work.*

Mary Prince. *Prince was the first Black British woman to escape from slavery and publish a record of her experiences. She escaped to England in 1828.*

Olaudah Equiano. *Also known as Gustavus Vassa. In 1789 Equiano published his book, 'The Interesting Life Olaudah Equiano'. The book was published 17 times and translated into both Dutch and German.*

Ottobah Cugoano. *Published 'Thoughts On The Evil And Wicked Traffic Of The Slaves And Commerce In Human Species' in 1787.*

Ignatious Sancho. *1729 - 80. Sancho was born on board a slave ship on its way to the Caribbean. He was taken to England at the age of two. Sancho served the Montague family and wrote poetry and music. He was also an art critic.*

David Walker *(1830). In Georgia bounties were placed on David Walker's head. Slave holders offered $10,000 for him dead.* **Walkers Appeal** *was openly read in the North and routinely smuggled South. Laws were passed suppressing the tract. State legislatures made it a crime to introduce or circulate literature advocating the overthrow of the system of slavery. Walker was a member of the Massachusetts General Coloured Association, founded in 1826 for racial betterment and slave abolition. He was the local agent for the RIGHTS of ALL. He had subscribed to the fund to purchase the freedom of George Horton of North Carolina and Phyllis Wheatley.*

Henry Highland Garnet *. 1815 - 1882. A former slave of Maryland, he escaped to New York City at the age of nine with his family. He became a Presbyterian Minister in 1842. He advocated armed resistance to slavery and issued a call to rebellion at the National Negro Convention. Active in politics after the civil war he worked for a time with the Freemen's Bureau and accepted an appointment as a U.S. Minister for Liberia.*

Fredrick Douglas. *Born in Maryland Virginia in 1817 he ran away. Formerly Fredrick Bailey, in 1836 he escaped to Baltimore disguised as a sailor. Assisted by David Ruggles the owner of a Black bookshop and a station on the 'underground', he reached his freedom in Massachusetts. In 1847 with Martin Delaney he published the 'Northern Star'. An internationally known Black abolitionists paper. In 1845 Douglas published the first of three autobiographies. Douglas served as a Marshal of Washington DC and was a Consul General to Haiti from 1889 to 1891. He died in 1895.*

REBELS, REBELLION
AND REVOLUTION

Sam Sharpe *led a slave rebellion in Montego Bay Jamaica in 1831. Sharpe was a literate slave and a lay Baptist preacher. Sharpe led a rebellion in which 20, 000 slaves refused to work. It took troops two months defeat them. Sharpe was executed on May 23rd 1832.*

Nanny Grigg. *A report by the Barbados Assembly on the 1816 rebellion noted that Nanny*

Grigg, a domestic slave, read the British and local papers and had been informing other slaves about events in Haiti and Britain.

Gabriel Prosser. August 1800 a Virginian slave set in motion a plot to attack and seize portions of Richmond City. Prosser mobilized over 1,000 slaves. The plot was betrayed before action took place. All involved were tried and hunged.

Nanny. The legend of Nanny of the Moroons has been passed down for many generations. Nanny was bought to Jamaica as a slave in the early 1700s. She ran away and went to live amongst the community of runaway slaves called the Maroons. Nanny became the leader of Blue Mountain Rebel Town. The rebels cultivated the land and organised society along the lines of the Asanties of Ghana. They raided plantations; in 1739 Nanny Town was captured; the leader, Cudjoe, signed a peace treaty with the British.

San Domingo. The encouragement for this slave rebellion came from a slave priest known as Boukman in 1791 when he was presiding over a service. He suggested that Black people should be paid for their work and given three days rest a week. On the 22nd of August slaves agreed to rebel. They killed 2,000 whites.

Toussaint L' Ouverture. Toussaint was an ex-slave of fifty who worked as a coach man and veterinary. He had learned to read and write and acquired an estate by marriage. Toussaint died in 1803 in the dungeons of the fortress of Joux in the Jura mountains, after months of brutal treatment. In 1795 the army led by Toussaint defeated the Spanish and in 1798 defeated the invading British army.

John Brown. In 1859 Brown, a messianic white abolitionist, carried out a raid on the government arsenal at Harpers Ferry in America. His intention was to seize weapons and to free slaves. Brown and others were captured, tried and executed. Brown said:

"I John Brown, am not quite certain that the crimes of this guilty land will never be purged away but with blood. I had, as I now think vainly, flattered myself that without very much blood shed it might be done."

Denmark Vessey. Vessey was a carpenter who purchased his freedom with the winnings from a lottery ticket. In 1822, 9,000 slaves and free Blacks from Charleston responded to Vassey's plot to liberate the city. The plot was betrayed to the authorities. Vassey was arrested and hunged.

Cripus Attucks. The slave Cripus Attucks was the first person to die fighting in the Boston Massacre of 1770, an event which marked the beginning of the American War of Independence.

Nat Turner. In 1829 and 1830 there were slave revolts in Louisiana and North Carolina. In 1831 Nat Turner and other slaves assassinated 60 whites. Troops put down the revolt, and over 100 slaves were killed. Turner was executed. Revolts in other Southern states followed.

Palmares. This is possibly the greatest slave revolt: it took place in Brazil. Slaves ran away and established two towns of about 5,000 people each in the forest in North East Brazil. In 1690 Palmares had a population of 20,000 people. In 1696 the republic of Palmares fell to the governor of Brazil. Rather than surrender the slaves fell to their death from cliffs. There were eight more slave revolts in Brazil between 1756 and 1835.

The Civil War. A total of 178,985 (10% of the Union army) of those who fought in the American Civil war were Black. Black soldiers were in segregated units led by white officers. By the end of the war 100 Blacks had received commissions. Martin Delaney was one of the first. Black women also served in the Union forces. Harriet Tubman became a scout. Susie King, who escaped from Georgia, became a nurse, laundress and teacher to the 54th Massachusetts and South Carolina Regiment in which her uncles and brothers served.

Important Quotes:

" I would rather die upon yonder gallows than live in slavery " - Sam Sharpe speaking to Reverend Bleby before his execution.

" Nanny and people like her helped to speed up the end of slavery. The slave rebellions that followed were inspired by Nanny and other freedom fighters. This fear of revolution was a major factor influencing the British to abolish slavery."

('Nanny of the Maroons' - Jamal Heritage Readers 1990)

IMAGES OF ABOLITION

Fig 1.

Abolitionists used a number of methods to make people aware of the inhumane nature of the slave trade. The production of pamphlets was the chosen method of the Quakers who preferred the spoken and written word as a means of opposing slavery. John Woolman's *'Some Considerations On The Keeping Of Negroes'*, which was produced in 1754 and sold 10,000 copies; John Wesley's *'Thoughts Upon Slavery'* and John Ramsay's *'An Essay On The Treatment and Conversion of African Slaves In The British Sugar Colonies'* are examples of abolitionist literature from the mid eighteenth century. The first visual materials to come from the abolitionists came after the creation of The Society for effecting The Abolition of The Slave Trade which was formed in 1787. Commissioned through the Society, Josiah Wedgewood employed one of his modellers at his Staffordshire pottery factory

to make a relief of the seal for production as a cameo (see fig 5). The seal was to show an African in chains in a *'suppliant posture'* and have the motto *"Am I not a Man and a Brother?"* As with Biard's painting, the cameo seal was deemed to be a success. It was able to convey far more than either the written or spoken word and had the ability, in its simplicity, to appeal to those who held Christian sentiments and believed in equality for all mankind. Some cameos were inlaid with gold, others were embedded into the lids of snuff boxes and ladies wore them in bracelets and as pins for their hair Such ornaments identified their wearers as members of a concerned elite and, in some instances, as active abolitionists. To others they became mere fashion accessories with their significance being all but lost. Mayhew describes the typical amulets and cameos of the time in *'London Labour and The London Poor'* (1651):

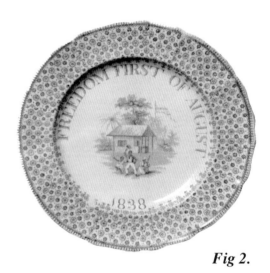

Fig 2.

Fig 3.

"a Negro with tracts in his hand, and a placard upon his breast, upon which was a woodcut of a black man, kneeling, his wrists heavily chained, his arms held high in supplication, and round the picture, forming a sort of proscenium or frame, the words: 'Am I not a Man and a brother?'"

But how are we to read these images? What did they say about African people and their ability to take their destiny into their own hands? What do the images say about the relationship between the slave and the liberator? The

Fig 4. African is often shown naked, Hugh Honour says of this that,

".......(African) nudity is both idealistic and realistic, classical and modern, heroic and pathetic. A nude figure, according to current artistic notions, signified the essential nobility and freedom of man, divested of all deceptive externals, as nature made him.... the posture is equally telling. Black figures had previously knelt in both secular and religious art, notably as servant or suppliants. But the pose could denote simple gratitude as well".

But, we are left with a contradiction still. That of the African in the pose of *"simple gratitude"*. We are presented with an interpretation of the African being thankful to the abolitionists, god, and Britannia for giving back to him that which he had initially - but lost when he became a slave - his freedom. Such images as those in figures 1-8 could never be seen as wholly positive, (though they did serve a purpose}, because Black submission and indebtedness is always implicit, and often explicitly taken for granted. Thus:

" It was the abolitionist emblem, that most well intentioned and commendatory of all black images, which came to crystallize and enshrine the idea of pathetic, docile subservience and Black inferiority ." Honour (ibid).

It is well recognised that the kneeling posture had discriminatory implications at a time when members of the upper class did not kneel when praying. It would, therefore, be accurate to describe the kneeling image of the African as negative, for not only does it express the image of the Black suppliant, but also white superiority.

Fig 5.

As all the illustrations in this section show, the theme of the Black suppliant was to remain in evidence throughout the period of the abolition, and well past it and on into the art of the 20th century and into more modern forms of communication up until the present day.

Phrases such as *"these unfortunate people"*, *" this unhappy class of mankind"*, *"these wretched African"*, and *"our poor Black brothers"*, however well meaning, served to stamp on the perceptions of the British a stereotyped view of the African: a view which was to gain momentum after the abolition of the slave trade with the expansion of the British Empire and the development of 'new' ideas, particularly in the sciences in Victorian Britain. These issues are explored in more detail in *'Slavery and Ideology - a Legacy of The Past'*.

Fig 6.

Fig 7

Fig 8

Fig 9

Fig 10.

FIGURES 1-10

(**1**) Abolitionists' coin. (**2**) Commemorative plate *"Freedom First of August"* 1838 (**3**) Detail from bronze relief on the Gutenberg Monument - City of Strasbourg *"Les bienfaits de l'imprimerie en Afrique"*. (**4**) Wedgewood Medallion for The Society for Effecting The Abolition of The Slave Trade -*"Am I not a man and a Brother ?"* (**5**) Abolitionist coin - *"What so ever ye would that men should do to you, do ye so to them."* (**6**) French abolitionist engraving showing the personification of France, the crowned woman, giving Black men and women their freedom - *" La cause des esclaves negres"* 1789. (**7**) Britannia, justice and the law are shown here, along with a bust of an abolitionists, as the mainstay of the abolition of slavery. (**8**) *The standard abolitionists' pose, "Am I not a Man and a Brother?"* (**9**) William Wilberforce, antislavery campaigner, Wilberforce Museum, Hull. (**10**) William Roscoe. A Liverpool Abolitionist and antislavery campaigner.

119

BLACK RESITANCE AND REBELLION

*T*eachers should provide the information on this section from Part One to pupils and students as background information. They should also be encouraged to carry out further research into Black resistance and rebellion and build on the knowledge gained from Section Seven, *'Black Abolitionists and The Abolition Of The Slave Trade'*.

The main aim of this section is to look closely at the role played by Black people in the abolition of slavery, as this is often omitted in other sources. It is particularly important that pupils and students are aware of:

* *Black abolitionists;*
* *resistance during the Middle Passage;*
* *how Black people made plantation societies unworkable;*
* *the San Domingue Revolution;*
* *the Maroons;*
* *protesters in Britain.*

a) Read through the account of the San Domingue Revolution and, using additional information, write your own account of it. In your account you should pay particular attention to the following:

* *What stimulated the revolution and how did events in other parts of the world have a bearing on it?*
* *Who lead the revolution?*
* *What impact did it have on slavery?*
* *Explain what the slaves were fighting for.*

b) Read through the account of the activities of the Maroons and answer the following questions:

* *how did the Maroons make the planta tion system unsustainable?*
* *when was the "first big recorded out break" of slaves in Jamaica?*
* *How did the Maroons survive and what was their relationship with those who remained slaves?*
* *As time passed there were lots of myths and legends created about the activities of the Maroons, but we do know of some of them by name. Name two Maroon leaders and find out about their lives and achievements;*
* *Explain how the British finally "put down" the Maroons.*

PLANTATION SOCIETY

No-one opposed slavery more than the slaves themselves and there are countless examples of their extraordinary actions and the determination of those who refused to accept the status of slave. Pupils and students should examine the pictures which illustrate plantation life in the Caribbean in the 1700s. They should answer the following questions:

* *What activities are the slaves involved in?*
* *Why were Black people used as slaves in the Caribbean?*
* *What goods were produced?*
* *What evidence is there from the pictures that slaves were treated badly?*

Pupils and students should be given the opportunity to read through a number of accounts of plantation life. They should be able to answer the following questions:

* *What was the most common form of protest against slavery in the Caribbean?*
* *How did Africans use their culture, songs and language, to protest against slavery?*
* *Name as many ways as you can, used by slaves, to halt or slow down production in the Caribbean.*

ESCAPEES AND FREEMEN

Escapes of slaves were common in the Caribbean, America and England. We know this by the number of advertisements used which described runaway slaves and offered rewards for their capture. Pupils and students should read through the section on *Escapees And Freemen"* (Part One) and answer the following questions:

* *How did Black people use "negro spirituals" to pass on messages to runaway slaves? Give examples of the songs and explain their hidden meanings.*
* *Explain what the 'underground railroad' was and how it worked.*
* *Why did Black escapees make their way to Canada?*
* *Where were the Exeter Halls and why were they important?*
* *Find out more information about the free slaves who toured venues like the Exeter Halls to tell about their experiences of slavery and how cruel and unjust the system was.*

RUNAWAYS

As stated, it was common to offer rewards for runaway slaves. Owners were eager to get their slaves back because they often became invaluable to the smooth running of a plantation or an estate. Also, if a slave was successful in running away this could have an impact on those who remained, encouraging them to try and secure their own freedom. Find out more about plantation life.

PLANTATION LIFE

From the documented evidence it is clear that plantation life was a cruel and harsh experience. Slaves were often treated badly and punished for the slightest misdemeanour.

* *What do you think were the most common offences?*
* *How were the slaves punished?*
* *For which offences would slaves be most severely punished?*

Teachers should encourage pupils and students to carry out follow up work. They should be encouraged to explore Black Resistance and Rebellion, and Plantation Life as part of a cross-curricular theme. Subjects such as English, Art and Geography would support such a theme.

Fig 1.

Fig 2.

Fig 3.

Fig 4.

Figs 1 and 2. Two views of Toussaint L' Ouver-
ture - leader of the Saint Domingue Revolution.
In 1797 he became the Commander of the
united French Revolutionary Army.
Fig 3. *Leonard Parkinson, Maroon Captain.*
Fig 4. *Maroon Warrior.*

The San Domingo Revolution

The most famous slave revolt started in 1791 in the French colony of San Domingue which became the so-called *'Negro State of Haiti'*. In 1789, the colony of San Domingue supplied two thirds of the overseas trade of France and was the greatest individual market for the slave trade. As James states,

> *"it was the greatest individual market for the European slave trade. It was an integral part of the economic life of the age, the greatest colony in the world, the prize of France and the envy of every other imperialist nation."* (Ibid)

However, in 1789 the French Revolution began with its battle cry of *"Liberty, Equality, Fraternity."* This cry was heard in the French colonies in which liberty, equality and fraternity did not exist. As in other European colonies in the West Indies, in San Domingo there were a number of distinct social groups: a hierarchy which was rigidly defined in terms of skin colouration. There were the wealthy and powerful whites, the *"grands blancs"*; there were the free people of colour, at the time described as coloureds and Blacks; and there were the slaves. The freed coloureds and Blacks were not, though, in a position to enjoy the same opportunities or have the same rights as their white counterparts. Similarly there were some educated and relatively wealthy coloureds who, socially and economically speaking, were in a better position than some poor whites.

When the French Revolution began, these economic, political and social differences were to be the focus upon which the San Domingue Revolution would be set, with the liberty and equality of Black people taking centre stage. Douglas (ibid) sums up the impetus for the revolution thus:

> *"In 1791 the revolutionary government in France announced that in the French colonies coloured people born of free parents should have equal political rights as whites. The whites in St. Domingue refused to accept this, and fighting began between whites and freed coloureds. Then, as whites and coloureds were fighting it out, the slaves revolted."*

This became a long-standing struggle for freedom in which the slaves of San Domingo began to rely on the leadership of Toussaint L' Ouverture.

Toussaint L' Ouverture was born a slave on the Breda plantation in the northern plain. When he joined the revolution it was as a physician, but before long he proved himself to be a very able commander and a great leader of men. He was also an excellent horseman.

Toussaint L' Ouverture

Public Flogging

PLANTATION LIFE

Life on most plantations was a harsh and cruel existence with slaves being publicly flogged for the slightest misdemeanour.

Slave quarters were simple huts made from wattle, daub and thatch. Some island assemblies passed regulations which stipulated that slave quarters could only consist of one room . Life for the slave was as basic as it could possibly be.

Plantation owners kept stock books which recorded the names of all the slaves on a plantation, what their activities consisted of, their age and the quality of their health. Owners also kept detailed records of slave punishments. Typically slaves would be punished for attempting to escape, for speaking back to their owners and for remembering, and practising African customs and traditions.

Slaves on the plantations were classified according to the work that they did;, most slaves spent some time as field labourers working in labourer gangs. New slaves would usually be 'seasoned' in these gangs while the owner, or overseer, assessed their skills. As slaves became elderly they would often go back to the field gangs to take up lighter work.

The slave driver had permission to use the whip on any slave, as did the ' Johnny Jumper', another slave, who would often be called on to carry out a whipping (see illustrations). Each planter had domestic slaves to serve his family as maids, cooks, butlers, gardeners and coachmen. Sometimes the domestic slaves were looked on as being more fortunate than the field slaves. Generally speaking their work was less harsh and their privileges were greater, as they were for the skilled slaves and the artisans. Close proximity with the masters family did, however, have its down-side. The Black butler being a convenient scapegoat for the anger of the planter and the maid for his sexual desires. And as Claypole notes, the work of the domestic slave was often degrading:

> " ... *many of the tasks they had to do were humiliating, especially when they were serving one of the planter's children. One young mistress was described as having three slaves attending her when she took her afternoon nap; two to fan her face and one to lightly scratch her feet. To add to the difficulties of their position they usually had to live in a compound near the great house and away from the other slaves who often treated them as outcasts". ('Caribbean Story ')*

Many slaves were not attached to plantations, they were hired. They belonged to their master who would rent them out. In addition there were the slaves who formed part of unskilled jobbing gangs which belonged to slave contractors and small land owners. They were hired out to do the work that could not be done by regular slaves. This work was often the most dangerous and back-breaking and involved the risk of injury or death. Working at crushing cane whilst exposed to the cogs and pulleys of the machinery was a particularly dangerous task that slaves often had to undertake. Slaves usually worked for about sixteen hours. Their day started at around 4.00am. Work was often done in accordance with a timed rota so that chickens and other live stock would be fed and cleaned out first. This was followed by 'roll call' at day light when the day's tasks were be assigned. There would be a short break before lunch, a two hour break in the afternoon and work again until sun down when they would be allowed to go back into their 'homes'.

Sugar Mill

The cycle of cultivating sugar cane began in the spring. Huge channels, about 6 in. deep, had to be dug into the ground. Once the field was planted the gang was made to weed, hoe, replant and manure the cane holes.

Once the cane was fully grown a shift system would be bought into operation with teams of slaves cutting the cane, while others processed it in the factories. The work in the factories, or mills, was dreaded even more than the backbreaking work of cutting the cane (see illustration). Factory work was hot and dangerous as the cane had to be fed into the crushing rollers of the juice extracting machines by hand:

> *"... there was an axe hanging by to cut off tired fingers which became caught up in the rollers. In the boiling house slaves suffered terribly from burns while stoking the furnaces and ladling the boiling sugar from copper to copper." Claypole (ibid).*

INSTRUMENTS OF TORTURE AND PUNISHMENT

Figure 5. A metal collar and padlock around the neck of a slave girl.

Figure 6. An iron mask to prevent the slave from talking or eating. There were several types of mask, all of which would have made it particularly difficult for the wearer to breathe.

Figure 7. A metal spiked collar. These came in several forms, but they all served the same purpose to prevent the slave from running away. Sometimes such collars would be so heavy that the wearer would be hardly able to move. If s/he were to attempt escape there would be little likelihood of success (the long spikes creating an obstruction) and the wearer could be immediately identified.

Figure 8. A pair of leg shackles - there were many types of leg and arm shackles, almost as individual as the owners and traders. They were all, however, designed for the same purpose, to restrict movement and prevent escape. Restrict movement they did, with the bar of leg shackles typically being only a matter of inches in length.

Figure 9. A public flogging - note the onlooker. Public floggings were a part of everyday life in the Caribbean and in the Americas. All illustrations of them have at least two things in common: the onlookers, who regularly came to observe (in the case of slaves, they were made to observe as a form of deterrent) and the use of a Black man ' Jumper' or 'Johnny Jumper' to administer the punishment.

Back ground image: Slaves digging channels for sugar cane.

125

Fig 5

Fig 6.

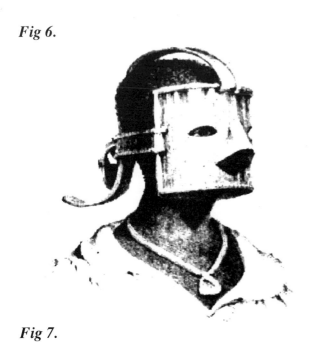

Fig 7.

"For the least fault the slaves recieved the harshest punishment. In 1685 the Negro Code authorised whipping, and in 1702 one colonist, a Marquis, thought any punishment which demanded more than 100 blows of the whip was serious enough to be handed over to the authorities... there was no ingenuity that fear or a depraved mind could not devise which was not employed to break their spirits and satisfy the lust and resentment of their owners and guardians - irons on the hands and feet, blocks of wood that the slaves had to drag behind them wherever they went, the tin-plate mask which was designed to stop the slaves eating the sugar cane, the iron collar." **CLR James** *'The Black Jacobins'.*

Fig 8.

Fig 9.

126

Fredrick Douglas

Fredrick Douglas was one of the most influential Black abolitionists. He was born a slave on a Maryland plantation around 1817, and escaped to Massachusetts in 1838. By 1842 he was a popular speaker at meetings organised by the Anti-Slavery Society. *"I appear before the immense assembly this evening as a thief and a robber"* were his opening remarks at one meeting. *"I stole this head, these limbs, this body from master and ran off with them."* In 1845 Douglas published a book describing his life as a slave, *'Narrative of The Life of Fredrick Douglas'*. This book conveyed in graphic terms the horrors of slavery and plantation life. It sold over 30,000 copies. In 1847 he became the leader of the New England Anti-Slavery Society and launched his newspaper, the *'North Star'* - so called because 'passengers' on the underground railroad travelled at night following the North Star. He spent nearly two years in Britain addressing large audiences throughout the country. He approved of violent uprising but declined to take part in John Brown's attack on the Federal arsenal at Harper's Ferry in 1859.

Cinque

Cinque and La Amistad

In the spring of 1839 Cinque, or Singbe, son of a Mende chief in Sierra Lione was seized, sold to Portuguese slavers and shipped off to Cuba. At Havana, Cinque and about 50 others were bought by two Spaniards who charted the Amistad to carry the slaves to Principle. Cinque led a mutiny on La Amistad, taking himself and his companions from one Cuban port to another in June 1839. He and his companions had managed to overcome the crew, killing the captain and the cook - they intended to sail to Africa. But the steersman, one of the Spaniards who was kept alive, headed the ship North. 63 days later La Amistad arrived in Long Island where it was boarded by officials of the United States Navy.

The mutineers were promptly imprisoned and the Spanish authorities demanded that they be tried for piracy. In addition their owners sued for their return. Newspapers were filled with articles about the case of La Amistad and interest was generated amongst the abolitionists who argued that the Africans had been kidnapped and that they had the same rights as other free people to use force in order to obtain their freedom.

Cinque and his companions were ably defended by lawyers who were abolitionists, amongst them was a Yale professor who managed to locate a Mende sailor who acted as the translator in court. When the case eventually passed to the Supreme court in March 1841, John Quincy Adams, former President, secured their acquittal by arguing that the slave trade had been declared illegal by Spain as well as the United States and that all men had the natural right to freedom. Quincy's final summation lasted for eight and one half hours. The court case proceedings lasted all winter and public opinion was divided as to the African's right to freedom. Cinque gave a passionate speech in his native tongue, this helped swing the verdict in favour of him and his companions.

As the case passed through the courts, its significance in the general context of slavery became apparent. But defenders were careful to insist that their aim was only to secure the release of Cinque and his companions and their return to Africa.

Whilst still in prison, the men and women from the La Amistad were given Christian instruction and after their release they were obliged to perform in churches, singing hymns and quoting the scriptures in English to raise funds for their return journey home. Their return was organised by the American Missionary Association which established a station in the Mende country.

La Amistad

Henry Highland Garnet

James Forten

Henry Highland Garnet. Garnet was a former Maryland slave, like many other Black abolitionists such as Douglas. He escaped to New York with his family when he was nine. In 1835 Garnet enrolled in the New Hampshire Noyes Academy. Garnet, however, had to leave the academy after a number of attacks were made on it by those opposed to the fact that it was integrated. He completed his studies in a theological institution near Utica, New York, and became a minister.

Sojourner Truth

Garnet became convinced that armed resistance was the only answer to slavery. He delivered a *"call to rebellion"* at the National Negro Convention in 1843. *"Strike for your lives and liberties"* he called to the nation's slaves. *"Rather die freemen than live to be slaves, remember you are four millions."*

In the Autumn of 1859, Garnet expressed hope that the end of slavery was near: *" I believe the sky is brightening, and though I may not live to see it, the day is not distant when, from the Atlantic to the Pacific, from Maine to California, the shouts of redeemed millions shall be heard."*

James Forten (1766 - 1842). Born a freeman in Philadelphia, Forten made a prosperous living servicing ships in his own dry dock. Forten gave generously to the antislavery cause. Among the first to proclaim that all men were biologically equal, irrespective of racial origin, he advocated women's rights, temperance and world peace. Forten produced a pamphlet in 1817 which opposed a consideration which was being taken in Pennsylvania to ban the employment of free Blacks: *" Has the god who made the white man and the black left any record declaring us a different species?"* He asked. *"...and should we not then*

Richard Ansdell - *'Hunted Slaves'* 1861. Liverpool Walker Art Gallery.

**Theodor Kaufmann - *'On To Liberty'* 1867,
New York Metropolitan Museum Of Modern Art**

enjoy the same liberty and be protected by the same laws?"

In 1833 Forten, alongside other abolitionists, organised the American Anti-Slavery Society.

Sojourner Truth (1797 - 1883). Sojourner Truth was an inspired orator, yet she never learned to read or write. Born a slave with the name Isabella Baumfree in New York, she was forced to marry an older slave and bore five children, three of whom were sold.

Truth escaped from slavery in 1828. She became known as a preacher while working as a domestic in New York. In 1843 she dedicated her life to preaching, taking the name Sojourner Truth. *" The lord gave me Truth because I was to declare truth unto other people ."*

Sojourner delivered her best-known speech at an 1851 Ohio women's rights convention. In a deep voice which resonated with her first master's Dutch accent she declared: *" Look at me! Look at my arm.. I could work as much and eat as much as a man - when I could get it - and bear the lash as well! And ain't I a woman?"*

After slavery Sojourner Truth committed herself to helping former slaves to find homes and employment.

130

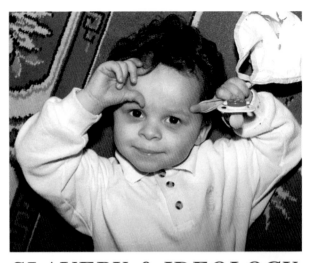

SLAVERY & IDEOLOGY
THE PROPAGANDA OF
THE SLAVE TRADE

The word 'propaganda' is used to describe methods of persuading people to think about things in certain ways. The intention is to make people *feel* deeply instead of thinking carefully. The propagandist usually shows only *one* side of an argument. The propagandist does not allow you to look at things in logical ways or encourage you to think about other people's opinions.

The reason why people sometimes use propaganda is because it is in their interest to do so, particularly if they need to defend something or justify their action. Slavery is a good case in point. Rich merchants, slave owners and captains of slave ships, in order to try and justify the cruel trade that made them wealthy, spread propaganda so that many people did not know the true horror of slavery.

PROPAGANDA AND THE STORY OF 'CURSED CHUS'

George Best, a sailor who had an economic interest in the slave trade, wrote that Black people were descendants from the cursed Chus. The original story is from the Bible in Genesis 9 and 10. The story goes that after the great flood Ham had looked upon his father's nakedness as he lay drunk in a tent, but that Noah's other two sons, Shem and Japheth, had covered their father with out looking at him. When Noah woke he cursed Cannan, son of Ham, saying that he would be a *"servant of servants"* unto his brothers. But what does this have to do with African slaves and justifying the slave trade? Some writers believe that probably over a very long time the story was supported by the ancient association of heat with sensuality (1) and by the fact that the sub-Sahara Africans had been enslaved by Europeans since ancient times. The fact that the story lingered on is also probably connected with the negative associations that people had with the word Black and the feeling that Blackness could not be any thing but a curse. We also have to remember that George Best was in the business of spreading propaganda and if he could show, or have people believe, that Africans were cursed and that they deserved to be enslaved then there would be few speaking out against slavery. We also have to remember that in the 17th century there was no mass communication and that myths abounded as to what people in different parts of the world looked like. There were differing perceptions as to how the world really looked and how far you could travel before you encountered strange man-eating creatures and the like. Most British people did not know what Black people really looked like and many people could not read or afford the few newspapers which were available. Even if they could read, it would be unlikely that the newspapers or books would be written by Black slaves, though this was to change in the 18th century when people like Olaudah Equiano wrote and gave public speeches on the evils of the slave trade. Best knew that if he could make people in Britain think that Black people were bad, then he could pretend that slavery was a sort of punishment, so that people would perhaps care less about the dreadful way that slaves were treated.

QUESTIONS
a) Find out more about the story of chus (also known as Ham).
b) Why was it in George Best's interest to pretend that Black people were cursed?
c) Think of a modern day, or recent, situation in which an individual, or group, has used propaganda to put their point across. Remember that during slavery there was no mass media, or mass communication. With your modern example explain the role of the media.

Cetawayo - Leader of the Zulus

By the late 19th century racism had gained a 'scientific respectability'. Images of Black people were created in order to support the notion of the superiority of one people, namely white, over Black.

In the late 19th century the Europeans were able to conquer Africa due to technological advancement, particularly in relation to weaponry and the machine gun. During the Zulu wars warriors were massacred by Gatling guns: they made an heroic stand at Ulindi, but they were defeated.

Cetawayo, king of the Zulus, was captured and exiled to Cape Town. He made a visit to London in 1888. Cetawayo was a patient and tolerant leader. He had pledged friendship with the British and had no intentions of making war on them. But because of the Zulu tradition of training men to be a strong fighting warrior force they resisted the British.

At the battle of Ulindi 10 British soldiers were killed and 60 were wounded, 1500 Zulus lost their lives during the battle, others died after the battle and many more were injured.

IMAGES OF CETAWAYO

Look carefully at the different depictions of Cetawayo. Look at the two photographs and then at the drawing (figure 3). Consider the following:

a) What does the expression on the face of the chief in the cartoon tell you? Write down what you think after discussing it with members of a small group.

b) In the cartoon picture look at the way Cetawayo is dressed and the ornaments around his neck and body. What sort of a man do you think he is? Do you think he appears to be kind and gentle? Write down your opinion after discussing it with your group or a teacher.

c) Now look at the two photographs of Cetawayo. Figure 1 shows Cetawayo after his capture by the British, figure 2 shows him as the king of the Zulus. Judging by the photographs, does Cetawayo look like an evil man , a kind man or just an ordinary Black man? Discuss this with your group and then write down what you think.

d) Did your opining of the cartoon and the photographs differ? Explain your answer.

e) If you agree that there are differences between the cartoon and the photographs then explain what vested interest the cartoonist (or the cartoonist's sponsor) might have had in depicting Cetawayo as a mythical and stereotyped character. What did the cartoonist want us to think about Cetawayo?

Fig 1.

Fig 2.

132

Fig 3

PLANTOCRACY AND PSEUDO-SCIENTIFIC PROPAGANDA

*T*he earliest language for the justification of slavery was undoubtedly that of the slavers and the West Indian planters they supplied. During the eighteenth century, promoting and sustaining not only a popular negative image of Black people, but also the notion of their debased humanity, was essential to the commercial success of the Slave Trade, holding public indignation at bay and strengthening the hand of the pro-slavery lobby in Parliament.

At the beginning of the nineteenth century, the education of the poor in Britain was viewed with suspicion owing to fears of insurrection of the sort which was prevalent in France. Education could nevertheless be a useful medium to combat subversiveness in used as a carefully controlled weapon. Although popular education in England and Wales would have to wait for the Forster Education Act of 1870, education with its religious base proved a useful medium to spread the creed of the slave lobby by use of biblical texts which appear to give divine validation to their ideas.

Education at the beginning of the nineteenth century though not yet universal in Britain, was nevertheless used to aid the spread of ideas about Black people as evil and debased creations. Notions of the bible and its apocryphal embellishments, such as that of George Best, (mentioned in the accompanying activities), were to be found early in the days of the slave trade.

A new language for the perpetuation of racist attitudes relating to people of African decent was to be the pseudo-scientific racism of the late nineteenth century; a more determined descendant of earlier attempts to 'prove' the rectitude of prevailing attitudes towards Black people by attempting to find a basis in science, so typical of the Victorian 'Age of Discovery', to support and supersede the earlier religious justification.

The idea of 'racial hierarchy' was established with northern whites at the top and African Blacks at the bottom with all other gradations, based on degree of pigmentation, in between.

a) Read through the above section and define the following:

* *The pro-slavery lobby ;*
* *West Indian Planters;*
* *pseudo-scientific;*
* *indignation;*
* *fears of insurrection;*
* *combat subversiveness;*
* *divine validation;*
* *dehumanised creatures;*
* *rectitude of prevailing attitudes;*
* *religious justification;*
* *'racial hierarchy'.*

b) Find out more information on the role that science played in making differences between people on the basis of their skin colour, physical features, skull size, height etc. Remember that we should view all theories critically because, in relation to slavery, they were all used to justify a particular point of view: in this instance, the superiority of one group of people over another.

133

READING AN IMAGE

The following exercise should be applied to all images and photographs in this and all other previous sections. It will help to stimulate responses and discussion among pupils and students. Answers can be written down or talked through using brief sentences or key words.

DESCRIPTION

How would you describe the image generally?
Who and what is in the picture?
What do you think is happening?
Where is it or where might it be?

ANALYSIS

What sequence of events might have led up to the scene in the picture?
What might it lead to?
What aspects of the image do you feel are unclear?
Do you have any questions about these aspects?
What do you imagine the feelings of the people in the picture to be?
What personal feelings does the image evoke in you?

RELATIONSHIP BETWEEN THE PICTURE AND REALITY

What issues does the image raise in your mind?
What problems do you think arise?
What do you think causes the problems?

SEARCH FOR SOLUTIONS

How can we solve these problems?
What opportunities are there for us to make things better or become part of the solution?
What will we as individuals and as a group commit ourselves to do?

The transformation of people from passive observers to active participants who can analyse then act, is the key.

EXAMINATION OF CHILDREN'S COMICS

For this project it is necessary to obtain a set of children's comics, the illustrated cartoon style, from a mainstream newsagents such as W.H.Smith or John Menzies, for a particular day, covering a broad age band. Up to about 20 are available which can be distributed to the group - either one each or one between two.

Participants are asked to count how many stories there are in each comic and then to examine how many have Black characters in them

Next, they should consider what roles the Black characters play e.g., lead or hero, speaking part, positive or negative, the quality of the illustration and so on, so that an analysis is carried out.

For example, in 1985 a study published in 'Black and White Media Show Book' (1) revealed that out of 274 stories in 23 comics, no less than 250 were exclusively white. Of the 24 with Black characters:

*   9 presented them as violent, stupid or grotesque;*
*   a further 10 were in the background with little or no personality, no dialogue and drawn as white with shading;*
*   4 more had minor roles with dialogue;*
*   the one remaining Black character was ' Mister T ' from the ' A Team ' with stereotyped dialogue and exotic dress.*

The conclusion was that people of African, Caribbean, Asian, Chinese, Arab, Japanese or Indigenous American origin were presented in a stereotyped and racist way or were omitted altogether.

Is the situation any better in the 1990's ? This project will allow you to judge for yourselves.

BEANO 1985

The following images and text are a small selection typical of those which were in mass circulation in Britain in the 1950's, 60' and 70' and which would have been absorbed by parents of today's school children. They continue to have an impact on domestic racial ideologies.

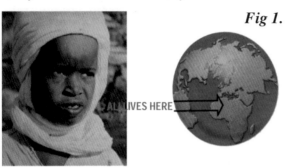

Fig 1.

Fig 2

Fig 3

HERE ARE TWO STRANGE PEOPLE

" Ali lives where it is hot and dry
Abdul lives where it is hot and wet..
Because of this they are strange to one another.
Because of this they are also strange to you.
In this book you will meet many more strange
people from strange lands."

Fig 4.

Fig 5.

Fig 6.

Fig 6a.

Fig1. A detail from the first page of a school book *'Real Life Geographers: Book 1 Strange Peoples'*. Published in 1966 and used in Liverpool schools in the 1970's. Almost everyone in the book is Black. Illustration features one of the "strange" people. Fig 2&3. Two headings from the story and cartoon features *'Chicks Own Annual'* 1956. Fig 4. Four of sixteen images from the story and stick-in series *'Races of The World'*. The text includes references which describe Europeans as highly civilized and Africans as primitive, and refers to:

"..a new world to which three Spanish sailing ships came and ....civilization." Figs 5, 6 and 6a are example of stereotyped images from the illustrated *'Ten Little Nigger Boys'* published by Nelson in the 1950's.

135

Representations of people of African origin in the British media in the 1980's and 90's are almost exclusively restricted to sport, entertainment, fashion/sexuality, war, famine and dehumanised caricature. Below are some examples.

Fig 1.

Fig 2.

Fig 3.

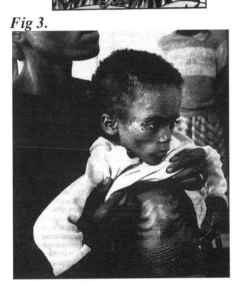

Fig 4.

Fig 5.

Fig 6.

Fig 7.

Fig 8.

Fig 9.

Fig 10.

Fig 11.

Fig 12.

Fig 13.

Negative Images Nourish Racism

" Most analyses of white-black relationships overlook the influence of images in mass culture upon racism in society. The conscious or unconscious acceptance of the stereotyped image of black people is partly responsible for the persistence of prejudices and racism." Exhibition notes from 'White on Black - Images of Blacks in Western Popular Culture'. 1990.

Fig 1. Casette tape cover for children's stories 1994 *'Billy Bumble's Favourite Tales'*.

Fig 2. Liverpool Echo May 12th 1987. Illustration to accompany letters supporting images of the golliwog.

Fig 3. *Observer Magazine* January 1994. *" ...desperate parents bring their malnourished children to hospital paediatric ward."*

Fig 4. *Sunday Times Magazine* September 1991.

Fig 5. *Liverpool Echo* July 1987. Cartoon depiction relating to the signing of John Barnes to Liverpool F.C. John Barnes was the first Black player transferred to Liverpool. Brian Moore is a football commentator.

Fig 6.   Mr 'T' of T.V programme *'The 'A' Team'* in *'VS Talking People'* August 1990.

Fig 7. Daley Thompson - Lucozade advert 1990's.

Fig 8.   Detail from *'Ellesse'* clothing and footware advertisement.   *Sunday Mirror Magazine* September 1991.

Fig 9.   Pop Singer Lionel Ritchie. Sunday supplement.

Fig 10. Ugandan children in *'New African'*   May 1986.

Fig 11. Benetton advert 1980's & 90's.

Fig 12. Racial caricature on the cover of Youth Training Scheme (YTS) brochure for Liverpool and Sefton published by Manpower Services Commission (MSC) 1984-85.

Fig 13. Sweet wrapper - Trebor Ltd England 1980's.

BORN TO BE $O£D

Poem by Abdul Salam

Born to be sold in Liverpool,
A child of the times,
destined to struggle
Within three lines.
A triangular prison   5
Is where I reside,
Out of sight
Out of mind
A problem tied
With a racist bind   10
Frontlines, Breadlines, Deadlines:
Testimony of the Truth,
Pressure in the triangle
Fuels a circle of disputes,

With the 'perfect ideology'   15
That doesn't really care,
continues lacing
Most of our lives
With poverty and despair.
A promise of a future   20
Where we rarely have a care
Living happy ever after
In safe hands
Free from fear.

Of all the people   25
Why my people?
Why should this be?
Is it we don't care?
Is it we don't see?

Issues raised today   30
Are crimes of History.
Capitalist Freedom and Democracy
Ebbed the tide of slavery,
Drowning all who fell before it
In the name of Liberty;   35
Sowing seeds of destruction,
Breaking up Communities,
Harvesting our Production
Baptised as commodities,
Ensuring enslavement   40
With the Lies
That seal treaties.

Aspirations for Advancement
Truly depend on you,
Understanding Columbus,   45
The significance of '1492';
there would be no celebration
Without the sale of you.

No European expansion,
No pseudo Christian Jew;   50
God almighty
would have saved us
From Columbus and his crew,
Man's existence through evolvement
The conduit, the Human Race,   55
Immersed in the need
Which we all associate.
Creating 'Races' in the plural
Is the catalyst of Hate.

There's new hope   60
Forming in the triangle:
It holds a place
For you, for me.
When you coincide
With a moment in time   65
forged way back in history,
That moment now gathers
Momentum,
Determination,
The need to be free.   70
Recognition will Enlighten
All people
Who take the time out to see.
The trade that died
A long time ago   75
Is alive and kicking and free
World Bank, IMF, UN and Tall Ships
Do little to Emancipate Me.

That which gives life's breath
To Liverpool   80
Came from Overseas.
To some it's just a memory
To others - the stench of disease
The dismemberment
Of African family.   85

Eurocentric Greed,
Superb in its Execution,
Stealing: African skins
African minds, African Souls.
Envisage the perfect Solution   90
As the Industrial Revolution Unfolds:
Africans fuel for millers' wheels,
Turning cotton buds into Gold.
Employment for the Masses,
Countless millions to   95
Others, Untold,
Dedicated Liverpool City fathers
Soaked in the blood
Of the People
Of the Globe: 100
Our pain, our suffering
Time will not ease
Racism remains Today.
A KILLING DISEASE.

BY ABDUL SALAM GAYLE

Some examples of questions related to the poem to stimulate further discussion and deeper understanding of *'BORN TO BE $0£D'*:

1   What evidence is there in the poem to suggest the identity or origins of the author ?

2   Why do you think the poet used the symbols $ and £ in the title ?

3   What do you feel the author means in lines 4 and 5 ?

4   What do you think is meant by *"out of sight, out of mind"* [lines 7 and 8] ?

5   What is meant by the *'lines'* described in line 11 ?

6   Reflecting on the irony in the use of the expression *"perfect ideology"*, what do you think is implied in lines 21 to 24 ?

7   What was the significance of 1992 [line 46]?

8   What does line 58 refer to ?

9   What do the initials IMF and UN stand for, in line 77?

Why do you think that the author does not feel emancipated by them and the others named in that line ?

10   Research and name some of the Liverpool City Fathers [line 97]?

SOME ANSWERS

1   *Line 6 "where I reside"; line 18 "our lives", line 26 - "my people; line 28, 29 "we"; line 52 "us": all suggest that the writer is of African descent and resident in Liverpool.*

2   *$ and £ are the currency symbols of the dollar, USA and pound sterling, Britain, the two capitalist beneficiaries of transatlantic slavery.*

3   *Local - Granby Triangle, Liverpool 8, denotes an area of the city where the largest population of African settlers and their descendants resided. Globally - the links between Britain, Africa and USA.*

4   *The oldest Black community in Britain and one of the oldest in Europe yet hardly recognised or represented: e.g. in city centre shops virtually no Black workers; out of 4000 school teachers only 30 are Black, and only 5 grew up in Liverpool.*

5   *Frontlines: invisible barrier sets boundary of conflict and survival eg policing policies. Breadlines: economic insecurity of family unit coupled with aspirational apathy. Deadlines: drug addiction, alcoholism, violence, gangwarfare, innocent victims.*

6   *Empty promises and hypocrisy of political parties*

7   *Quincentenary of Columbus' exploits, celebrated by some, opposed by others, with Tall Ships transatlantic extravaganza ending in Liverpool.*

8   *There is One Race - the Human Race, which has been separated into nations, tribes, communities, families, cultures by competition and 'divide & rule' policies of capitalists and colonisers.*

9   *International Monetary Fund and United Nations.*

BIBLIOGRAPHY

1) Rae Alexander 'Racist and Sexist Images in children's books'.

2) Nayaba Aghedon   Comment on 'Black Markets' (Exhibition).

3) Alkalimat 'Africa Before and After The Slave Trade'.

4) Imamu Amira Baraka   'Blues People: Negro Music In White America'.

5) Reverand Henry Bleby   'Death Struggles of Slavery'.

6) Edward Blyden   'Christianity, Islam and The Negro Race'.

7) Dorothy Broderick   'Images of The Black in Children's Fiction'.

8) W.G.B.H. Boston (Pub)   'African Americans'.

9) Encyclopaedia Britannica Vol 27, 15th Edition 1994.

10) Margaret Busby   'Daughters of Africa'.

11) G.Cameron & S.Cooke   'Liverpool, Capital Of The Slave Trade'.

12) Chambers Dictionary (1986).

13) William Claypole & John Robottom 'Caribbean Story - Book One: Foundation.'

14) Thomas Clarkeson 'Essays on Slavery and The Commerce of The Human Species'.

15) David Dabydene 'Hogarth's Blacks - Images of Blacks In Eighteenth Century English Art'.

16) Basil Davidson 'Discovering Africa's Past'.

17) Basil Davidson   'African Kingdoms'

18) Fredrick Douglas 'The Life and Times of Fredrick Douglas'.

19) Draft Proposals For The National Curriculum For History - July 1994.

20) P.Edwards & J.Walvin 'Black Personalities In The Era of The Slave Trade'.

21) Olaudah Equiano 'Interesting Narrative'.

22) Exhibition 'White on Black - Images of Black People in Western Popular Culture'.

23) James Ferguson   'Far From Paradise'.

24) Thomas Frazier 'Afro American History: Primary Sources'.

25) Peter Fryer 'Staying Power' - A History of Black People in Britain'.

26) Peter Fryer 'Black People In The British empire - An Introduction'.

27) Lord Gifford , Wally Brown & Ruth Bundy: The Gifford Inquiry 'Loosen The Shackles'.

28) Joanne Grant 'Black Protest: History, Documents & Analysis; 1619 to The Present'.

29) W.A. Green 'British Slave Emancipation: The Sugar Colonies and The Great Experiment 1830-65'.

30) Alex Haley 'Roots'.

31) Douglas Hall 'The Caribbean Experience - An Historic survey 1450-1960'.

32) Harraps Dictionary (1988).

33) Richard Hart 'Slaves Who Abolished Slavery' Volume 1.

34) P.Hulme & N.L. Whitehead 'Wild Majesty'.

35) Winthrop D. Jordon. ' The Blackness Without' - Reproduced in 'White Man's Burden'.

36) The Liverpool Chronicle - 1750s.

37) Liverpool Maritime Museum - Exhibition Text.

38) Thomas Lloyd-Jones 'Know Your Liverpool'. Walks in The City'.

39) D. MacRitchie 'Ancient And Modern Britons'.

40) Patrick Manning 'Slavery and African Life'.

41) David Milner Survey of Comics - Research in 1975.

42) CLR James 'The Black Jacobins - Toussaint L 'Ouverture And The Saint Domingue Revolution'.

43) Hans Koning 'Columbus - His Enterprise'.

44) William Mathieson 'Great Britain and The Slave Trade 1839-1865'.

45) Oxford English Dictionary (1989).

46) Oxford English Dictionary - illustrated - (1990).

47) Patrick Phillott 'Black Studies: Notes on African History'.

48) Oliver Ransford 'The Slave Trade'.

49) Anandi Ramamurthy 'Black Markets' (Exhibition).

50) J.A.Rogers 'Sex And Race' Volume 2.

51) Dicky Sam 'Liverpool and Slavery'

52) Sherlock, Parry & Maingot 'A Short History of The West Indies'.

53) M.Shinnie 'Ancient African Kingdoms'.

54) A.Shundel 'A History of The Aztecs and The Mayas'.

55) Fritz Spiegel (Foreword) 'Liverpool and Slavery'.

56) Dorothy Sterling 'The Making of An African American: Martin Robinson Delaney 1812-1885'.

57) Eric Williams 'From Columbus to Castro - A History of The Caribbean 1492-1969'.

58) Eric Williams 'Capitalism and Slavery'.

59) Gomer Williams 'Liverpool Slavers and Privateers - With an Account of The Liverpool Slave Trade'.

60) The Williamson's Advertiser August 20th 1756.

61) World Council of Churches 'Racism in Children's and School Text Books'.

62) Howard Zinn ' A Peoples History of The United States'.

ADDITIONAL REFERENCES PART TWO

1) Duncan Castlereagh - 'The Great Age of Exploration'. Readers Digest.

2) Susanne Everette 'The Slave Trade -An Ilustrated History of The Monsterous Evil'.

3) Hugh Honour 'The Image of The Black in Western Art'.

4) Ramsey Muir 'A History of Liverpool'.

5) *'The New Internationalist'. December 1991.*

6) *'Merseyside: Painters, People and Places'. Walker Art Gallery. Published by Merseyside County Council 1978.*

7) *Jamal Heritage Readers . 'Nanny of The Maroons'. Published 1990.*

8) *Mayhew. 'London Labour and The London Poor'.*

9) *'Real Life Geographies'. Published in 1966.*

10) *'Ten Little Nigger Boys'. Published by Nelson in the 1950's.*

The Black History Resource Working Group

BOOKS AND RESOURCES

*All books and resources over leaf with ISBNs and written information are available from **Liverpool City Council's Race Equality Management Team (REMT)**. For further information on all resources contact: REMT. Education Directorate, 22 Sir Thomas St., Liverpool L1 6BJ. Tel: 0151 225 2765/2886. Fax: 0151 225 3029. E.Mail: ga 14@ dial. pipex.com. Prices are exclusive of postage and packaging and are negotiable for bulk orders with special discounts to book suppliers and distributors.*

*All other resources are available from **Liverpool Anti-Racist Community Arts Association (LARCAA)**, a Black majority visual arts organization formed in 1988. Posters and posts cards featuring local artists range from 50p to £15.00 inc. postage. For further information about LARCAA exhibitions, graphic design and production, posters and photography telephone: 0151 709 0380; Fax 0151 708 6818 or write to 23 Clarence St., Liverpool L3 5TN*

'*Exploring History*'. Suitable for KS1 of the National Curriculum for History. A dual language text, Somali and English. First published 1993. Paper back format, full colour: £2.50

'*The Story of John Archer - Britain's First Black Lord Mayor*'. Suitable for KS1/2 of the National Curriculum for History. Book contains facts and details about John Archer's life with illustrations. ISBN: 0 952478916: £3.99

'*Slavery: An Introduction to The African Holocaust*' Suitable for anyone interested in the history and legacy of the slave trade, with special emphasis on KS3 of the National Curriculum for History. Paperback with over 150 black and white and colour images. First published in 1995. ISBN: 0 9524789 00. £14.92

'*Slavery: An Introduction to The African Holocaust*'. Revised hardback edition. New and improved with additional colour images, 150 pages. Published in June 1997. ISBN: 0 952478935. £16.99

'*People of The African Diaspora In Non-Traditional Roles*' - Poster pack. Eight high quality large full colour posters featuring barristers, architects, fire fighters, members of the police force etc. with statistics, facts and figures: £15.00.

'The Same. But Different'. Suitable for KS1 of the National Curriculum for Science. Text in three languages: Somali, Arabic and English. First published in 1996. Hardback format with full colour throughout. ISBN:0 95244789 27: £4.99